ACTOR'S ALCHEMY

FINDING THE GOLD IN THE SCRIPT

ALSO BY BRUCE MILLER

ACTOR'S ALCHEMY

FINDING THE GOLD IN THE SCRIPT

BRUCE MILLER

AN IMPRINT OF HAL LEONARD CORPORATION
NEW YORK

Published in 2011 by Limelight Editions
An Imprint of Hal Leonard Corporation
7777 West Bluemound Road
Milwaukee, WI 53213

Trade Book Division Editorial Offices
33 Plymouth Street, Montclair, NJ 07042

Parts of this book first appeared in some form in *Dramatics* magazine and in the journal *Teaching Theatre*.

Grateful acknowledgment is made to Samuel French, Inc. for permission to reprint EYE TO EYE by Chris Graybill. Copyright © 1989, 1992 by Christopher Graybill.

CAUTION: Professionals and amateurs are hereby warned that "EYE TO EYE" being fully protected under the copyright laws of the United States of America, the British Commonwealth countries, including Canada, and the other countries of the Copyright Union, is subject to a royalty. All rights, including professional, amateur, motion picture, recitation, public reading, radio, television and cable broadcasting, and the rights of translation into foreign languages, are strictly reserved. Any inquiry regarding the availability of performance rights, or the purchase of individual copies of the authorized acting edition, must be directed to Samuel French Inc., 45 West 25 Street, NY, NY 10010 with other locations in Hollywood.

Printed in the United States of America
Book design by Kristina Rolander

Library of Congress Cataloging-in-Publication Data

Miller, Bruce J.
  Actor's alchemy : finding the gold in the script / Bruce Miller.
    p. cm.
  Includes bibliographical references.
  ISBN 978-0-87910-383-5 (pbk.)
  1. Acting. 2. Theater--Semiotics. I. Title.
  PN2061.M463 2011
  792.02'8023--dc22
                          2010050878

www.limelighteditions.com

TO MY FAMILY AND FRIENDS —
WHO HAVE ALWAYS BELIEVED IN ME

CONTENTS

INTRODUCTION

This book on acting will not attempt to be comprehensive. You may not find everything you ever wanted to know about acting and how to do it at this location. Instead, this book will focus on the elements of acting craft that the typical actor struggles with the most and, not surprisingly, effectively deals with the least. These aspects of the craft are what most actors spend the least time developing in a specific, thoughtful manner during their training. These vital elements are always mentioned in class and assumed to be a part of the preparation process of every actor. But too often in training, these elements are assumed to be aspects of the craft better learned elsewhere. They are not considered to be appropriate subjects to practice in class in the same way many other skills are.

Actors work on their voices and physicality—often in specialized classes dedicated to those elements. Then they bring what they have learned to the acting class and into the rehearsal studio. Actors practice finding truthful behavior and work toward more emotional depth on a daily basis in their acting classes. These are considered part of their essential ongoing development. It is understood that actors need to work on these elements of craft continuously if they are to ripen into skilled artists in their field.

Acting classes themselves tend to focus on elements of the craft concerned with the self, on the relationship between characters developed onstage, or on the moment-to-moment give-and-take between actors. Performers learn to ask themselves questions like: How do I feel at this moment? How can I conjure that feeling? What action works best for me here? How can I deepen my connection with my scene partner, or use that object on the stage to stimulate real emotion? All good questions to ask, no doubt.

But too often the work actors bring to class demonstrates an inability to make choices based on what the script tells them they must show or do. This failure often leads to work onstage that obscures the story and meaning of the play and makes the actors look somehow deficient. Unfortunately, much of the time actors never even realize that this keeps them and their work from fully succeeding.

This book will examine the relationship between the script and what an actor ultimately does onstage or onscreen. When actors learn to use their scripts in a specific and analytical way, they more easily find the choices that will work to solve the problems of the scene and that bring their elusive characters to life. Too often, actors take for granted this essential part of their skill development or leave it for others to nurture. It is part of the script-analysis class that is all too general and all too short, or, for some of you who are reading this book, may never be presented at all.

Analysis and synthesis skills play only a small role in many acting classes, and a class that is more often simply about "doing" or "feeling," disconnected from the script, seldom features those skills as more than tangential subjects. As a result, many young actors — and even working ones, for that matter — never adequately develop the ability to analyze a script and connect it to the work they put onstage.

Many actors never learn to integrate the script effectively with their work because of the way they have been trained. In many programs, a great deal of time is spent doing exercises having nothing to do with using a script. Students may be told they are not yet ready to handle the playwright's words. I know that my own training began that way. As I look back now, I realize that many of the exercises I did early in my training were good ones, but their value was lost because the exercises were not properly connected to the more sophisticated scripted work that would ultimately become the source of most of what I did as an actor.

However, the biggest contributor to the gap between script and actor today may be the fact that too many actors are aliterate. That is not to say that they can't read; it's more that they don't like to do it, and don't know how to do it effectively. Many actors simply don't want to be bothered with this part of acting. Actors often think of reading as something they must get through in order to do the real work — acting on the stage. For whatever reason, they want to distance themselves from the playwright and the script they are working from. Many actors consider the script to be the jumping-off point for their own work rather than the wellspring for all that they will eventually do. In my opinion, this approach is a mistake.

Disconnecting from the script is like beginning a journey across unknown territory without a map and passing by the well without filling the water barrel. Actors who do so believe they'll intuitively find their way across the vast acting prairie and bump into that single oasis just when they need to. Sounds pretty ridiculous when thought of in these terms, right? Perhaps this sounds a little like you.

The script is the actor's natural wellspring and map. It is a gold mine waiting to be discovered. If mined properly, it will make you, as an actor, very rich. A good script tells a story effectively, and that is exactly what an audience wants to see. Keeping this fact in mind is critical for the actor who is going to act compellingly. Actors simply must learn to read their maps carefully if they are to find their way through a scene or play effectively. Actors must also learn to turn what they find in their scripts into actions they can play for an audience. This requires imagination, of course, but more importantly, it requires the ability to read, analyze, and use a little common sense. Most of this can be learned — if you have the will to do so.

Most good actors constantly use their brains to make the best dramatic choices at every moment of their work. Only after actors make and explore these choices does artistic freedom come, and this freedom permits the seeming spontaneity apparent in fine acting.

Learning how to find these choices in the script and converting those choices into actions that the audience understands is what this book is all about. Good acting requires making big choices and taking risks, but the choices have to be connected to the good story the playwright has set down. The actor must first understand that story, and then understand his or her part in its telling. The actor must then be able to convert that understanding into choices that the audience can see. Only when properly prepared with the choices that spring from the script are actors ready to listen and interact with each other onstage and be in the moment. Only then will they will be able to tell the stories they have uncovered compellingly and believably.

ACTOR'S ALCHEMY

FINDING THE GOLD IN THE SCRIPT

ACTING ON THE SCRIPT

ON THE SUBJECT OF ACTING, PEOPLE USUALLY FALL INTO one of two categories. Either they can't believe how hard acting is and would never dare attempt it themselves, or they think it's easy and believe they could do it better than most of the people they see doing it for big bucks. Those who think it's hard usually think so for all the wrong reasons. They think it's hard because it takes all that memorizing, or it's hard because it requires getting up in front of others and exposing themselves to the critical response of watching eyes.

These issues are certainly a part of the acting process, but neither approaches the core of what constitutes an actor's art and craft. Those who think that acting is easy believe it's simply a matter of saying the lines and being real — whatever that means — and being real seems easy enough, since all of us are able to fabricate a bit when the need arises. Of course, everyone agrees that some really great actors are able to unleash those really big emotions and be believable at the same time. Those tasks, however, can be reserved for the select few, the real geniuses, and as long as the roles requiring that kind of talent are avoided, then just about anybody can act.

Actually, it is probably true that everyone can act — to some degree. Most of us do it every day in real life. It's called social acting, and for those of us who make our way successfully in society, it is a skill that must be learned.

John pretends that he likes his boss whenever they're together even though he really detests the pompous jerk. Joan feigns sympathy for her least favorite student, who has just had his nose punched in by a kid who feels the same way she does. But by bestowing a ration of faked sympathy, this teacher manages to play her role well. Sara pretends that she doesn't mind the fact that her best friend got the part she so badly wanted. She keeps her head held high because pride dictates that she must. These behavioral choices mask our real feelings, and when we do the masking well, our honesty and integrity never come into question. We lie like truth — because this kind of mostly harmless lie gets us what we want or need, or keeps us from losing the ground in life we have already gained.

Most of us begin learning our acting skills at an early age through play. When we were kids and learned to "play pretend," we were essentially doing what every actor does — behaving believably under fictional circumstances. When our big sister played the doctor and came at us with the needle, we reacted appropriately in our role as patient. We turned our heads away and bit our lips apprehensively, or we ran out the door screaming, depending on whether we chose to follow our real-life inclinations, or the choice we were making for our character. When the kid down the street shot me with his poison dart gun, I died a slow, painful death, once the poison set in. During our playtime, we lived the lives of astronauts, the pioneers who headed west, or the perfect lives of Ken and Barbie. We used our imaginations and what we knew about those characters and circumstances to make the stories we played out come alive. And we were brilliant.

But as we move toward adulthood, self-consciousness and social pressures begin to cut into our abilities to tap our imaginations in these fearless ways. Some of us, however, retain that ability to build fabrications whenever necessary. Those of us willing and able to lie like truth make up stories and deliver them effectively as the need arises. We lie to the gullible principal to cover our butts, we fabricate the sob story to the cop to justify our speeding, or we pretend to be the big man on campus to impress that hot girl in our math class. Others of us, less able to employ the bald-faced lie to gain advantage, still engage in the role playing required to get ahead. We pretend to like what we don't, we put on that smile when we feel like crying, and we do many things that we don't want to in order to please those we feel we need to. All of us present different versions of ourselves in different circumstances every day. We play one role for our parents, another for our teachers and coaches, yet another for our friends and colleagues. We put on our specialized masks and take them off as needed. And each of us has accumulated many of those masks in our trunks for specific situational use. I venture to guess that many of us tailor the self we show to every social encounter we engage in.

So it really shouldn't shock us when the basketball player or wrestler takes off his hightops and successfully exchanges them for a fat role in a Hollywood movie, or when he so convincingly sells us a product on television. And it certainly shouldn't be any surprise when the singer or supermodel makes the jump from the radio or runway to the silver screen. Whether it's J.Lo or Brooke Shields, Shaq or The Rock, each is taking his or her accumulated social acting skills and attempting the leap into professional acting. How successful each will be, commercially and artistically, varies from name to name. And occasionally, when a talent emerges like that belonging to a Cameron Diaz, we might even see an actor with the emotional depth and range of skills belonging to a legitimate artist.

But good acting requires more than a highly developed sense of social acting and an ability to memorize lines. And a lack of self-consciousness alone will not a good actor make. Nor is the ability to portray strong emotions necessarily synonymous with what most would consider good acting.

The standard definition of *acting* goes something like this: behaving believably under fictional circumstances. As the definition stands, this is exactly what Shaq is doing when he pitches a particular product to us. The fictional circumstances are that he really believes that the beer he is selling is fabulous and he so badly wants us to partake in the joy of product that he has discovered. If Shaq says his lines in a somewhat believable manner, he is a success. But even if he sounds totally fake, the mere fact that he is Shaq, believable in his delivery or not, fulfills the conventions of advertising that we are used to. He gets his big fat paycheck for acting as himself, and some of us go out and buy the product.

But as an audience we are less generous when Shaq is cast in a role in a movie. We judge him or a Michael Jordan far more harshly when either must meet the obligations of a story. Years ago, supermodel and child actor Brooke Shields found her acting career come to a screeching halt when as a teenager she was cast in lead roles in which she was dreadful. Beauty notwithstanding, her physical awkwardness and disengaged delivery sidetracked her acting career for several years. Her acting was not believable, and the story she was hired to tell sank under her. More recently, The Rock parlayed his wrestling fame into lead roles, including one in the recent remake of *Walking Tall* and his first film, a spinoff of *The Mummy* called *The Scorpion King*. Cast as a warrior in that film, The Rock found himself in a box-office success, because he was already a hot show-business commodity and the role he took on could be played as The Rock. The difference in personality between a comic-book warrior king in an action flick and a wrestling superstar may not be a great one, and to a large extent The Rock was being asked to do little more than what he had already done professionally. In *Walking Tall,* he actually had to act a little, and, though stiffly, he managed to do so.

But what if The Rock had been cast in the lead role of Maximus, in *Gladiator,* the part played by Russell Crowe? At face value, this would seem to be a legitimate possibility—the two performers might seem at first glance to be the same type. Physically The Rock would be perfect for Maximus, the world's greatest gladiator, and what a professional wrestler does and what a gladiator does have points in common, to say the least. So why not?

In spite of physical similarities, you're probably laughing at the ridiculousness of the suggestion. Consider the work Crowe did in the film *A Beautiful Mind,* a role that won him an Academy Award. During the course of the film, Crowe made a complex acting journey that covered many years and difficult changes emotionally, psychologically, and physically. And we saw all this, though much of the time there were no words for Crowe to use to communicate his thoughts and feelings to us. But somehow he did.

All right, you're thinking, that particular role is obviously out of the league that The Rock can currently play in. But why not the Maximus role in *Gladiator*? Couldn't The Rock have pulled that off? The answer is maybe, but at great loss artistically, and probably commercially, as well.

Crowe gave the film and the part a magnitude and dimension that The Rock—and, for that matter, many legitimate actors—could not have brought to it. And the reason for this is that Russell Crowe is a fine, fine actor; and a good actor, though it often goes unnoticed by an audience of untrained eyes, brings to the work a body of choices that add color and clarity to what the writer has put down on paper in the script. The good actor seamlessly tells the story that the writer sets out to tell and does so believably and compellingly. An actor like Russell Crowe, no matter how easy he may make it look, has a body of craft that helps him choose and execute acting choices that add to the basic groundwork the writer provides.

If you are at the beginning of your acting training, or if you are an actor who does not currently feel that you have a tangible craft—a set of tools for making acting choices that will work effectively in any acting situation—then the preceding paragraph may be news to you. I know that whenever I ask beginning actors about the work they are doing at any given moment, they invariably want to tell me about their characters' *feelings*. And often when I'm working with capable professional actors who can produce believable work anytime they pick up a script, even they cannot always account for the choices they make while developing a scene. Nor can they connect the choices they produce with the script they are working from. This is not tangible craft, and this is not a technique that will faithfully serve them or the scripts they work from.

On the other hand, when actors make their primary focus what their characters are doing—not what they are feeling—and derive the choices they make from the script they work from, then the audience will intuit what their characters feel, and that audience is far more likely to understand why those characters do what they do during the course of the play or film. That is, of course, if those actions are well selected and executed and serve the script. Only through the appropriate and combined actions of all the characters in a play does the story laid out in that script gets effectively told.

An audience may, for a short time, appreciate the fact that an actor can conjure up seemingly real tears and cry at will, or muster up enough anger to single-handedly destroy an enemy army. But the fact remains that once these abilities have been shared with an audience, the audience quickly grows weary with them and turns its attention elsewhere. An audience can never see directly into the hearts and minds of a play's characters. They can determine a character's thoughts and feelings only as a result of what those characters do and say. What an audience wants, what it has come to the theatre for in the first place, is the story.

It is an actor's job, then, to tell stories, clearly, dramatically, and believably. The best acting will always serve the play in which the actor performs. It is not enough that an actor comes off well to an audience. A good actor must come to accept his or her responsibility for bringing to life the work of the playwright being produced. When the play is worthy, the actor will invariably best serve himself and the production by paying close attention to what the playwright has provided.

The definition of *good acting*, then, is "acting that is believable and tells the best possible story while serving the script." This definition will serve as the cornerstone for this book, and it can serve as a compass for you from here on in—in any acting situation in which you find yourself.

SERVING THE SCRIPT AND DRAWING FROM IT

Reliably good acting results from the active connection between the actor and his or her source material—the script. At first you might think that this seems like a constriction that will compromise your creativity, but it will actually have the opposite effect. By making choices that come from an analysis of the script, you will enhance your ability to act effectively. Here's what I mean.

Suppose I asked you to write an essay. The suggestion alone might be cause for panic for some readers. For those of you not inclined to the writing life, the task may seem daunting. In fact, for some of you, totally debilitating. No parameters that have been laid out, and infinite possibility can easily lead to stagnation. But suppose instead I had asked you to write an essay on acting. That would help you somewhat, because you are no longer staring at a night sky that seems endless. Now suppose I asked you to write an essay on your favorite actor and why he or she is so. Ideas for your essay are now congealing, and even if the essay has not begun to write itself, you have a direction in which to head.

That's how it works with acting, as well. Knowing what to do onstage or for the camera can be as daunting as writing an essay—if you don't go into it with a clear-cut set of parameters. Telling the story contained in the script gives you such parameters. In fact, when carefully read, a script gives you the blueprint of the building you must construct, so to speak. The secret is in learning how to read the blueprint and discover the steps it takes to create the building. If you want to act well and dependably, as an actor you must make choices based on the story being told in the script.

CONFLICT

Stories start with conflict, the engine of drama. Playwrights and screenwriters do not write with the hope of someday finding their work included in a literary anthology. They write because they want to see their work produced for the stage or screen. The better the story they produce, the more likely their goal will be met. Audiences go to the theater or to the movies to see a good story. Any good story starts with a conflict, and conflict sustains the action of a story from the time the conflict is introduced to its resolution at the end of the play or movie. Even when characters seem to be just talking, the good dramatist is moving the action of the story forward somehow. That means conflict is always present. It is your job to recognize that conflict and use it to propel the story forward—at all times. If no conflict is present, then the more conflict you can create, the more interesting you and the story will be. When conflict is apparent, the bigger you can make that conflict, the better for the story and for your work. If you're working with another actor onstage or onscreen, rest assured that something is going on between your character and that other character, and whatever it is, it must be related to the C word, conflict.

Two people onstage together, just talking. What's wrong with this picture? The word "just" is a giveaway. If any dramatic description begins with a minimizing word like "just," chances are you're headed for acting trouble. "Just" is a problem avoider, and as an actor you always want there to be a problem for your character to overcome. That's dramatic. That's the way the writer thinks, so if you find a way to minimize his or her craft, you're probably heading in the wrong direction.

Better to think like this: *Ah, two people onstage together—what's their conflict? If I find that conflict, I find the core of the scene, and I find something active to play in the scene.*

At the beginning of *Of Mice and Men,* George and Lennie are sitting around a campfire just talking. Except they're not. Through the playwright's craft, the good analyzer quickly realizes that a lot of conflict exists between George and Lennie because they have had a long and difficult history together, a history that precedes the opening of the play. Their history is, in actor

7

terms, their given circumstances. These given circumstances come out in the dialogue of the scene. The audience hears this background information for the first time, but George and Lennie are well aware of it. George wants to find peace, and Lennie wants, in his childlike mind, to have his every whim satisfied and satisfied now. These are the actions that the actors playing the characters must focus on. Lennie is the obstacle to George finding peace, and George is the obstacle to Lennie having his desires met. This dynamic comes out in the conflict of the scene—if the actors bring to the scene the buildup of their past experiences together. Overcoming obstacles provides conflict when actors playing characters go after their needs full-out, when they play their individual actions.

Without the conflict in evidence, the opening scene of *Of Mice and Men* is merely exposition and not dramatically interesting. With the given circumstances acknowledged by the actors at the play's opening, conflict can be played out. As a result, their characters' needs (objectives, actions, intentions), and therefore what they must do to obtain their goals, becomes clear, and who they are as characters quickly begins to emerge.

Here is another example that might be familiar to you. This one is from *The Glass Menagerie*—the scene between the gentleman caller and Laura. Is this a dull scene in which the two characters discuss old times and Laura shows Jim her glass collection? Or is it a scene in which a desperate girl tries to hook the man of her dreams, knowing that if she fails, it is all over for her? Is it a scene in which a polite but disinterested young man passes some idle time, or one in which he senses what is at stake for the girl and must find a way to extricate himself from the situation as gently but as quickly as possible? The difference in how you as an actor perceive the scene can mean all the difference in the world as to how you play the scene out. Even in the perception, the difference in the power of the story is quite obvious.

It should be growing clear to you now that in spite of the blueprint for the story that is provided by the writer, it remains your job as the actor to recognize that story and to flesh it out through the choices you make and execute as the actor playing the character. Simply relying on your instincts will not be enough most of the time. When the choices are infinite, reaching into the haystack and grabbing a handful of hay is likely not to produce any needles. The good actor knows where to reach, though what he or she pulls out will still provide enough surprises to keep all concerned more than busy.

ACTIONS, ACTIONS, ACTIONS

Even when you correctly decipher the story being played and choose actions that will serve the story, there remains the obligation to communicate that story clearly to an audience. Many actors, especially film actors, believe that if they feel the scene moment by moment, those feeling will be communicated directly and clearly to the audience. While it is true that the camera can pick up emotional nuances that would never be readable by an audience in the theatre, it is not necessarily true that the film audience picks up all that is intended simply because the actor is thinking it and feeling it. Nor is it true that what an actor naturally thinks and feels best reveals the unfolding story.

As an actor you must make choices objectively and find ways to communicate those choices to the audience. The primary tool for communicating with an audience is through the physical actions you choose to execute, and by the manner in which you execute them. An audience, in spite of what film actors sometimes think, cannot read minds and hearts, but they can extrapolate what those characters may be thinking and feeling from the actions they see characters carrying out, or by connecting what we see a character do with what we already know about him or her. Sometimes actors produce these clarifying physical actions naturally and spontaneously, but not always.

You must be willing to inspect and harvest the physical choices that come naturally to you, and keep the ones that work. They may be further amplified through repetition and rehearsal — making them more specific while keeping them seemingly natural. Where no physical actions naturally spring from the context intuitively, you must be willing to step outside your subjective, in-the-moment self and look at the work from the audience's perspective. This will lead you to think of what actions in the situation might communicate your character's thoughts and feelings to the audience. Then it becomes a matter of finding effective ways to execute those choices.

The Lennie who gulps his water from the creek in the opening scene from *Of Mice and Men* is a different Lennie than the one who carefully dips in his hand, trying to keep his sleeve from getting wet. The one who angrily demands that George tell him the story of the ranch and of the rabbits is a different creature than the one who pleads gently for the same story. The George who picks up after himself following his temper tantrum is different than the one who kicks the garbage viciously out of the way. The George who invests in the ranch story and is drawn into it despite himself is a far different George than the one who completes the story as he began it, grudgingly. The George and Lennie who physicalize their love for each other are different than the ones who avoid physical contact.

All of these actions, physical or psychological, either come spontaneously through the rehearsal process or have been invented by the actors to best serve the story as they perceive it. But each individual choice in combination with others makes for a slightly different set of moments, and ultimately for a different story being told, inhabited by characters unique to that specific production. Yes, the overall blueprint was provided by the playwright, but that particular *Of Mice and Men* will be like no other. And hopefully, the combination of choices made for that production will bring out the story provided by the playwright more clearly and compellingly than any that came before it.

LISTENING AND BEING IN THE MOMENT

In spite of the thought-to-action approach to acting that will be put forth in this book, the fact remains that in order to be *believable* onstage or on film — that third prong of the definition of good acting — it is necessary to be available and connected to your fellow actors at every moment you are onstage with them. No matter how brilliant your choices may be, acting in a vacuum will never make for good acting. Every preconceived acting choice must be adjusted to whatever actually happens prior to doing it onstage. If something fed to you by your partners onstage differs from what occurred in rehearsal, an adjustment must be made. If something has altered spontaneously during a performance, every good actor knows that an adjustment must be made. Reacting to what's going on in the moment creates the illusion of "happening for the first time," and it gives actors the chance to truly live in the moment. This is one of the reasons why no two performances of a play are ever quite the same. The story can be effectively told in an infinite number of ways, but acting without listening is not one of them.

The biggest difference between the acting of the talented high school actor and those with a higher level of training, and the biggest difference between the best film or stage actors and those clearly not of that league is often connected to the ability to listen. By listening I mean listening with all your senses. It means reacting to what is put before you. The best high school actors are often those who are deemed to be reliable performers. "No matter what," the compliment goes, "Johnny gives it that same money performance every time he sets foot onstage!" That's great, up to a point. But the fact is that sometimes this compliment means that in spite of whatever happens onstage that is new or different, Johnny will give that same performance, even if it means ignoring the multitude of changes that may occur from performance to performance. This concentration on what has been rehearsed is often admired in high school but becomes an Achilles heel to the development of a more sophisticated level of work demanded in the profession. The best acting does not seem performed. It seems spontaneous even when well rehearsed. Reacting in the moment gives acting the seeming spontaneity it demands.

Here are few examples of what I am talking about.

If you've ever been in an acting class, you've probably noticed how students are often very believable and exciting onstage when they are asked to do an improv. They have this uncanny ability to connect with their fellow actors and react in a moment, picking up on every vocal, verbal, and physical cue that comes their way. They are able to see everything that we can see and hear from our safe vantage point in the audience. But when these same actors are asked to read from a script, this seeming spontaneity and ability to react in moment-to-moment fashion almost completely disappears. The reason, of course, is that when they are improv-ing they focus on the other actors and on listening with all their senses, but when they do their scripted work they focus on the script and on what they will have to say next.

In scene-study class, I often ask student actors to improv a scene they can't seem to get a handle on. Invariably, when they manage to remove themselves from the obligations of focusing on what they will say next, many moment-to-moment discoveries start being made. Very often these step-by-step discoveries help the actors find their purpose in the scene and the story that eluded them when they were rehearsing. Of course, it is also true that when they attempt to go back to the scene as written, they sometimes lose much of what they learned in the improv—unless I force them to focus on each other rather than on the words they are struggling with. Since plays are not primarily about the words but rather about the story being told, the good actor has learned that dialogue is no more or less important than the other tools an actor must employ in order to effectively tell the story. Listening onstage is one of those tools.

Every actor who can read a script efficiently automatically begins to create a movie in his head—about what the scene will look like and sound like, and about how each scene should unfold and be played out. No two actors' movies will be alike. When actors come together to rehearse, they bring with them all the homework preparation they have done on their script. But since no two actors' mental movies are alike, each will have to give up aspects of his or her own movie and create, through the rehearsal process, a new, shared version. This new version will accommodate the actual give-and-take based on the choices being made by each actor, both prepared and spontaneous. Eventually, through the rehearsal process, all prepared choices will be forgotten because the rehearsal process will have ingrained them into the actor. They'll be there, but the actors will no longer have to think about them. Then the actors are fully available to be in the moment and create the magic that the best actors create.

In summary, then, acting is an amalgam of the following:

- reading and interpreting a script efficiently
- making choices that are exciting, believable, and tell the story effectively
- executing physically the choices decided upon so that they are clear and believable to an audience
- listening in the moment to create the illusion that all is unfolding for the first time

In the chapters that follow we will examine how these basic tools can be developed through hard work, common sense, and an ability to take and use feedback.

MINING FOR PHYSICAL ACTION

IN THE MOOD FOR A LITTLE CHALLENGE? OKAY. HERE'S A game of skill you can play alone, or with a group of actor friends. You'll need a stopwatch or clock and lots of talent. Stop reading until you've gathered your equipment and your friends, if you've opted for the group version. All set? All right, then, let's see how many of the emotions listed below you can muster and maintain for at least five seconds. You have a total of two minutes to conjure and maintain as many of them as you can. When you're ready, give yourself a "go," punch the clock, and start your emotional countdown! (Don't read beyond the list until you've played the game.)

romantic love	nervousness	exhaustion
anger	shyness	maternal love
joy	boredom	sympathy
hate	pain	lust
brotherly love	envy	sadness
disdain	shock	jealousy
ecstasy	embarrassment	

So, how did you do? Were you able to conjure up all the required emotions and feel them—I mean really feel them?

If you had some trouble doing so, believe me you're not alone. You might recall that Morales from *A Chorus Line* had her share of trouble conjuring up feelings and emotions from thin air, as well. In fact, it was only when her teacher Mr. Karp died that she could produce a legitimate emotional response. Now, if you who *were* able to conjure some or all of those emotions, the big question is—were your friends able to tell what the emotions were as you conjured them? If you played alone, you might want to try the contest again later—and this time do it in front of an audience of your peers. I'm warning you, though; no credit will be given unless your friends recognize the emotions you're feeling. It doesn't matter whether you really feel them or not, by the way. If your audience sees them, you get credit; if they don't, your work doesn't count. That, by the way, is also the case when you're acting in a play. Regardless of how it may have felt to you, the test is in the audience believing you feel it. After all, actors act for an audience.

You may have guessed by now that I'm being a little facetious with all of this. I'm trying to make a point here, and the point is that, as an actor, working with emotions directly can be very tricky business. When you try to conjure up an emotion like sadness or hate or melancholy directly, you may or may not hit pay dirt on any particular day. If, for instance, you've had a very bad day and feel like crying, being called upon to do so in an acting situation may pose no particular challenge. If, however, you've had a great day and are called upon to do so, it might be a completely different story.

Suppose you're in a play where you are expected get really angry at a particular moment, and you're just plain feeling too good? Your performance, and the play you're a part of, could be compromised. The money actor, the one most directors would want to hire or work with, is the one they can count on. The goods are there every performance no matter how that actor is feeling. That particular actor is the real pro. Acting must to be repeatable and controllable. Not that it has to be robotic; it can vary and change from one performance to the next, of course, but the goods have to be there when they are called for.

During my own early years as an actor, I had a teacher who at the time I thought was brilliant. He could turn dull work by an actor into something really special by playing with the actor's own emotions. I watched him on several occasions do personal, emotional work with an actor right in front of the class. If a character in a scene was extremely sad, for instance, because her mother had just died, he could take his actor on a personal emotional trip, and before he was finished, that actor was crying with sobs that came in waves. And just when that actor was on maximum emotional overdrive, my teacher would tell the actor to begin the scene. Very often the scene that followed was amazing—because real emotions were driving that scene. On more than one occasion I watched this teacher purposely tick off a vulnerable actor struggling with a scene—in order to conjure some anger that was consistent with the emotion called for in the scene being worked on. When my teacher felt the actor was truly ticked, the actor would be told to start the scene. Again, the scene was riveting—because it was charged with the actor's real feelings.

Now that I've got you psyched up, I should probably also tell you that when these actors put up their scene the following week, much of what we had seen the week before was no longer there. Worse, in many cases, we could see the actor working to recreate that emotion rather than playing the action of the scene from moment to moment. Don't get me wrong, some of the time with some actors, especially with advanced and very well-trained actors, this kind of approach to the work is very effective. Acting from the "inside" or from an emotional base has produced much legendary work—because it has been recorded for posterity on film, and we all know that the camera doesn't lie. The approach to acting being described was the one that Konstantin Stanislavski first explored and discusses in his work *The Actor Prepares*. But ultimately, his focus turned away from playing emotion—because it proved too unreliable for his purposes.

Besides being elusive, conjuring and playing emotions directly does not necessarily communicate clearly to an audience. Have you ever had the experience in class or during a performance in which you have really felt that you were on? But when it was time for the critique, the class or audience totally mistook what you were feeling, or didn't see anything going on at all? I know I have. There were many times when as a young actor I would leave the stage thinking I had really nailed it. I was totally one with my character; my character and I had totally merged; I had transcended myself and become. Then, when I hit the wings, still floating above the ground on my success, the stage manager's heavy paw would grab my shoulder and spin me around.

While looking directly into my triumphant eyes, he would ask the devastating question, "What the hell were you doing out there?"

"Acting," I would respond.

"Not tonight, you weren't!" he would exclaim without mercy.

So, if acting from emotion is so unreliable and so unclear, what are you supposed to do instead? The answer lies in what that same Stanislavski guy turned to when his "emotional truth" approach to acting let him down. What he did was turn to his theory of physical action. In short, the great Russian acting teacher came to believe that actors should rely on actions rather than emotions to communicate their part of the story being told. He came to feel that through a good process of thought, selection, and discovery through rehearsal, the actor could shape a performance physically that communicated clearly the characters' thoughts and emotions, and be reliably repeated at will. Physical actions are repeatable and controllable. They depend on nothing more than physically carrying them out. In addition, what Stanislavski learned was if the actor selected well, the physical actions carried out could inspire and even generate the emotions that were appropriate to the moment. Let's see how this works.

Take an emotion like hate, for example. Even if I could actually think of someone I literally hate (thank God, I can't) and tried to conjure up the feeling by using emotional memory like my former teacher did, it is doubtful that I could conjure so well that I could communicate my feeling to an audience watching. The emotion of hate, out of context, might prove very difficult to convey even if I could "reach right down to the bottom of my soul." I could, however, ask myself some questions, the answers to which might provide me with some physical action that could communicate my hatred. Suppose, for instance, I am playing Anne Frank, in a stage production of her life. I am thinking about Nazis and the loss of relatives and my former life. What might I do as Anne if such feelings struck me? Before I answer, I would have to ask myself about my *given circumstances* (the who, what, when, and where of my situation), and then I could come up with appropriate physical actions to show my feelings. I could rip up a picture of Adolf Hitler I found in an old newspaper, or draw a big X over his image with a heavy crayon in a forceful manner. I might even spit at the image in an ultimate gesture of contempt. The point is, I could find ways to communicate my feelings as Anne, ways consistent with her character that are clear, believable, and dramatic.

Now let's try an experiment. Find a piece of paper that you are willing to sacrifice to the cause. Pretend that on the paper there is a picture of Adolf Hitler. Now rip the paper as though you were Anne Frank. Continue reading after doing so.

If you committed to the action, you probably also generated some feeling recognizable as hatred. Your action generated feeling, and the feeling seemed real because you committed to it. Now try the exercise a second time before reading on.

It is likely that you were successful again, perhaps even more so than the first time—because you used what you learned the first time and improved your tearing technique for the second try. If you did this experiment with someone watching, he probably understood your action and totally believed you. He also probably understood the emotion behind your action, whether or not you actually felt it to your own satisfaction. This is what I mean when I declare that physical action is both controllable and reliable. You can conjure clearly when you want to and as many times as you want to—if you select and execute an appropriate physical action. Playing the emotion directly, and without a context, will not afford you the same reliability.

Now let's return to the list of emotions from the beginning of this chapter. Select several of the emotions listed and try to put each in a context. Some, you will quickly realize, are more difficult than others to find a context for and, therefore, to make clear. Jealousy, for instance, usually arises out of a specific series of previous incidents and involves one or more other people who created the framework for this feeling. Your job as an actor is to analyze every acting situation before you can come up with effective actions to play out. If you select an emotion that you know you cannot communicate for this exercise, make a wise acting choice and avoid using this emotion. There are plenty of others to choose from.

For now, stay within the framework of yourself. Don't try to be a character. Just think of a situation in which you actually experienced the emotion you select. Go through the list of given circumstances that were present at the time you felt this emotion. Where were you? What things were physically present at the time? Tables, chairs, outside, inside, kitchen, living room, schoolyard? When did this happen? How old were you? Time of year? Time of day? Et cetera. What actions might you have performed then, when you were younger, as opposed to now? Think of as many specifics as you can, and determine which of those specifics can help you define a series of actions that you might undertake to make clear the felt emotion.

Now jot down a series of actions that you executed at the time of the situation, keeping in mind the given circumstances; or if you can't remember what you actually did, jot down some actions you might have performed. When you have completed your notes, actually go through them step by step physically. After you have gone through the steps, think about what worked and what did not. Are there some details in your selected actions that you might have performed that you did not? Are there some details that you actually performed that did not work well for some reason? Can those actions be refined? Rethought? Thrown out?

Rethink your actions in these terms and make any necessary changes to improve the clarity and power of what you did the first time through.

Here is an example. When I was eighteen, I was called to my grandmother's house because my aunt could not wake her up. When I got through the door of her apartment, I immediately saw my grandma lying lifelessly on the couch. I remember slowly approaching her, standing over her, and then touching her hand and then her cheek. Both were ice cold. I thought she was dead. I backed away a few steps and turned to my aunt, and we hugged.

When I tried this set of physical actions on my own, I realized a number of things. First of all, in an exercise, I would not have my aunt available, so adjustments would have to be made. Further, I didn't remember doing anything in response to the coldness in my grandmother's hand and cheek, but when I went through the actions, I realized that, for story purposes, I needed to add some physical actions to show that her hands were cold. I chose to rush from hand to cheek, and to complete the sequence by feeling for a pulse and then slowly and carefully lowering her arm back into position. I then backed away until I caught the edge of a chair and slowly lowered myself into it. The net result, it seemed to me, communicated that my grandmother was indeed dead, and that my grief was beginning to overtake me. (My grandmother, as it turned out, was not dead at all, but merely sleeping deeply, and she lived many more energetic years. But I'll never forget the feelings aroused by this incident.)

Rethink your actions in these terms and make any necessary changes to improve the clarity and power of what you did the first time through.

When you are sure you have thought through and executed your series of actions as clearly and as strongly as you can, perform them for an audience and get feedback. Know that any comments about what was not clear are good comments. They are comments far more useful than simply being told that your work was great. These comments are the ones that will help you refine your work so that it will be even better the next time. This is the kind of feedback that you should want.

Now try the emotion through action again.

So, how did you do and what did you learn? In all probability, the work you performed was far clearer and more interesting than what you might have come up with by simply relying on an attempt to demonstrate emotion directly. This last time through you also had a road map for yourself—a list of actions written on paper that you could use, refine, and develop. This list you worked from actually has a name—the *physical action score*. Like the sheet music a musician uses, your physical action score provided you with a specific outline to keep your work clear and keep you on track. If you were well rehearsed, you were able to add to the basic score with your in-the-moment responses as you moved through your sequence. The emotions that the score reflected were probably evident to you and to the audience.

In the exercise just completed, I asked you to be yourself and concern yourself not with character, but with the use of physical actions that can help you develop character in the same way that it helped you develop and make clear emotion. "Becoming the character" is a phrase I often hear students use, but like playing emotion directly, it can be dangerous—sometimes leading to choices that hide rather than clarify the story being told. An actor in a play has a responsibility to make choices that serve the script by forwarding the overall story. Simply "being the character" does not necessarily fulfill this obligation. "Becoming the character" also sets up an expectation that you may not be able to fulfill. Becoming the character is not necessarily a requirement in order to perform well.

When I was a beginning actor, I would hear actors on talk shows discuss "becoming the character," and if the role was demanding, how playing this part so affected some actors that it actually drove them to the psychiatrist's couch. Robert Blake, the former star of *Baretta,* was one such actor, who made appearances on the television program *The Tonight Show* with Johnny Carson. Some actors do find it necessary to transform into their character, but that is not the case for many actors, and for those who need to, it can be dangerous. If like Robert Blake, it so consumes their life that they become mentally unstable, this road should not be taken. The onetime television and film star has been seen very little recently. He became prominent several years ago as a result of the coverage of his trial for killing his wife. He was convicted. You can decide what this all adds up to.

So if the actor does not aim to become the character, then what?

That's a cue to return to the great Stanislavski for a moment, and to his theories on physical action. The master acting teacher came to believe that in addition to portraying emotion, physical action could be used to reveal character, because he felt that action was often synonymous with character. Have you ever heard the expression that we are what we do? This old adage has direct bearing on the acting process, and it led Stanislavski to another great acting tool that has become a standard piece of equipment for the actor today — the use of "the magic if." When working on character action Stanislavski would ask his actors, "What would you do if you were this character in this situation?" Each of us behaves differently in a particular situation, and by isolating choices that the character we are playing might carry out, and then actually doing them, we can communicate character to an audience.

For example, suppose a character has just been told that his mother has died in a car crash? How might you react? I'm not asking how you would *feel*. The question is what would you *do*. Knowing myself, I think I might not react emotionally immediately. I'd probably turn away from the giver of this news, find a chair, and slowly sit down. Perhaps I would put my head in my hands and close my eyes. But that's just me. My father would leave the room quickly, go into his bedroom, and quietly close the door. My brother would find a wall and pound his fist on it. My sister would not react. She would just go to the television and turn it on. All of the responses I just described were fictional, but all could be legitimate reactions, and each suggests something about who the character doing them is.

We can take this idea a step further. Suppose all the members of my family react by going to the wall and hitting it. Even with the same general physical action, there is so much nuance to be found that the manner in which the action is carried out also can reveal character. My father slams the wall one time with an open palm in a clipped fashion. My football-player brother pounds on the wall with his fist several times as though with a hammer. My sister flays her open palms against the wall, totally out of control until she is exhausted. Again, each of these gestures tells us something different about who the character is — about what he thinks and about the nature of his feeling.

Here's another exercise to try out. Write down three descriptive paragraphs. In each, detail a particular character. Be specific, so that when the paragraph is completed you have some idea about who the character is. Once you have created a picture of each of these characters, perform a series of physical actions in which each responds to the information that his or her mother has died. Be sure that the physical actions are appropriate to that character and reveal his or her nature. Perform your physical-action scores for an audience and get feedback. Repeat as necessary.

Now try the exercise again with a list of historical or literary characters. Or, if you prefer, use a character from a play you are very familiar with. After you complete the exercise, ask yourself whether you felt character. If you committed to the action, and particularly if the action is not natural for you to do, you likely felt something akin to character. The actions, though alien to you personally, became comfortable when properly rehearsed. This, of course, is the key to much of the work we do as actors—doing it enough so that it becomes comfortable. Perhaps after enough rehearsing you might even start to feel like you are "becoming the character."

Now that you've got the hang of the exercise, you can do it with any character—one that you create, someone you know, a historical person, or a character from a novel or play. You can also change the piece of news brought in, so that the selected character and you, the actor, can experience a broad range of reaction possibilities. The point here is to develop your abilities to communicate emotions and to create character through the physical actions you select. The opportunities for creation are vast. So go do something.

Before closing this chapter, just a short anecdote. Some time ago I heard Mike Nichols, the great theatre and film director, interviewed on National Public Radio. He was promoting his HBO film *Wit*, based on the award-winning stage play by Margaret Edson. Nichols was asked by his interviewer if he found it difficult to translate a play essentially built on words and ideas into the visual medium of film. "Not at all," was his reply, because even in a play like *Wit*, the action speaks so much louder than the words. By way of example he described a scene from the play in which the main character, a renowned English literature professor dying of cancer, receives a hospital visit from her former mentor. The old professor, realizing that the patient is beyond the comfort of words, takes off her shoes and climbs into the hospital bed with her former student—to give comfort as a mother might to a child. She also begins reading *The Runaway Bunny*, a picture book about comfort and safety that she has just bought as a gift for her grandchildren. The simple act of her climbing into bed and reading a profoundly simple book dwarfs the metaphysical poetry of John Donne that has been quoted throughout the play. These actions instantly bring an audience to a state of sobbing. Such is the power of physical action. Your job as an actor is not to feel, but to get the audience to. That should be the bar we set for ourselves.

CHAPTER

THREE

DIGGING FOR
THE STORY

IMAGINE FOR A MOMENT THAT YOU ARE AT AN AUDITION and you have just been handed a sheet of paper on which you find the following dialogue:

A. Hello!
B. Hi.
A. Well. See ya.
B. Yeh. Bye.

So, what do you do? You're going to be called in to read in a few moments, and this is the script that they gave you. If you've been reading carefully up to this point, you know that the main themes thrown at you so far have been about using the script and finding the story. But there is no story in these lines, you're thinking. Wrong! There most definitely is—if you're willing to find one. And having a story to tell as you audition will serve you far better as an actor than just reading a bunch of lines. So find the story and find a way to look good as an actor.

We'll begin by looking at the lines themselves for clues. Since you and your scene partner are going to have to say them in the order in which they are written, let's assume that a sequence of cause-and-effect exists in their writing—that one line leads to another, because playwrights think that way. Something happens. What happens causes a reaction, which then causes something else to happen. This is the way plots work. This is the way most playwrights work, as well. Playwrights know that the audience is after a good story, so they write conscious of telling that story. If that is the case, then at least the bones of a story can be found at this archeological dig, so we must begin digging.

Without too much trouble, we can see that the sequence of lines begins with a greeting and a response—"Hello," "Hi." No problem so far. But then there is a "Well." The "well" can only suggest that something has happened between B's "Hi" and A's "Well" to elicit that response. What it is we do not know. At least we now have a clue to the potential unfolding story. Then A says, "See ya." Again, this line suggests that something must have happened, because the two characters, for whatever reason, are now ready to separate. What did happen between them? We'll never know from the lines themselves—there's just not enough information there—and since we have no previous scene, following scene, stage direction, commentary, or criticism to look to for clues, we simply have to settle for the fact that *something* happened.

This is a very important basic point about acting and playwriting. Very often, actors think that plays are about dialogue. Pick up the script—say the words, do the play. But that is a big misconception. Plays tell stories, true, but the dialogue is just one tool the playwright uses to tell that story. The words of the play are no more or less important than the other devices used to make the story unfold. What a character does is every bit as important as what she says. Since we have only bare-bones dialogue to work with, we can conclude that there must be hidden action to this story—action that the playwright has not provided. If it is not provided, then we must as actors invent that action; but as we do so, we must keep in mind that we are still responsible for justifying everything we say in terms of dialogue. In other words, any action we provide must be consistent with the words the playwright has given us. This is our job as actors as we tell the story.

Let's take another look at the dialogue.

A. Hello!
B. Hi.

A. Well. See ya.
B. Yeh. Bye.

Now that you're more familiar with the words of the script, what do you think the "Well" means, and how does that "Well" lead to the "See ya" that suggests a leave-taking? Of course, we don't know for sure, but we do know that we will have to invent action that somehow justifies our saying it. B then says, "Yeh," some sort of agreement with A's "See ya," and says, "Bye," himself.

The meaning of that "Well" is very important. It seems to be a response to something that has happened. The word itself has many definitions—from a hole in the ground where water is found, to a description of how you are doing. But neither of those meanings seems justified in the moment in the scene. It is most likely that the "Well" said here is the place-holding kind, the word we use when we're not sure what to say next. Given that something happened prior to the "Well," this use of the word can be justified and will add to this moment in the story. So then we have a "Well" that suggests an awkward moment followed by a kind of good-bye. Why an awkward moment? Something really interesting must have happened before that "Well" to create that awkward moment, right? This is good. We are beginning to have a suggestion of a story.

B agrees with a "Yeh" and then says, "Bye," himself. The logical question to ask is why does B say, "Yeh," before he says, "Bye"? Or better yet, why doesn't B simply say, "Bye?" You might be tempted to be flip here and simply say, "'Cause that's not what the playwright wrote." True as far as it goes, but in a play by a good playwright, we must assume that everything is there for a reason. If the playwright chose to write "Yeh," then there is a reason for it.

We need to ask ourselves why, and why "Yeh" specifically rather than "Yes" or some other affirmative. When do we use that particular construction? In the context it seems to suggest a less than wholehearted response—as though B doesn't really want to be hearing what A is saying. B's choice of "Bye" reinforces that theory. "Bye" in the context of our unfolding scenario seems small and not heartfelt. It seems as though it is a leave-taking word used when the speaker does not really want to be going. The character could have said, "*Hasta la vista,*" "Until we meet again," "Farewell," or "*Ciao.*" But the playwright gave B just a diminutive "Bye." We must assume that is exactly what the playwright meant. It follows, then, since we have no other information to go on, that something happened between the opening greeting and the leave-taking to make our characters reluctant to depart. It suggests to us that something big must have happened between our characters—the kind of big that can lead an actor to the telling of a good story.

So let's recap, based on our detective work. A and B greet each other. Something happens between them that causes them to not want to depart from each other. Then they say their departure salutations. That's all we know. But we now know far more than we knew before. What we know is also far more useful to us as actors. We have a foundation on which to build a story. We know the starting point and finishing point of the story. We also know that whatever happens in the middle causes the two characters to desire not to leave, although they say their farewells. Now we have an outline for a beginning, middle, and end—the necessary arc or throughline for any story.

The ambivalence about leaving suggests a conflict, and conflict is the engine of drama. It is the motor that powers any story. There are three kinds of conflict, essentially:

- Person against person
- Person against him- or herself
- Person against nature or society

Of the three, the most useful type of conflict for an actor and playwright is the first. Invariably, when two people are put onstage or onscreen, a conflict can be found between them. A person against him- or herself is the second most common and useful conflict for an actor. A character who can't decide what to do or which of several choices to commit to can prove very interesting, but this kind of conflict is much more difficult to convey to an audience than a direct person-to-person conflict. The nature conflict is most apparent in survival scenarios, and nature can usually be considered an obstacle to overcome. The character who is pitted against society is usually pitted against a series of individuals who represent that society. So bottom line, an actor will most often deal with the first two conflicts.

Whatever the type of conflict, without it, there is no story. And with it, you have a story fraught with dramatic potential. So, when A and B meet, something happens between them. They should or must leave each other, but they don't want to. What happens, and why? Those questions spark our curiosity, make us speculate, and cause us to want to fill in the blanks.

Before we further pursue our hunt for the story to be told, just a moment for some sidebar commentary. Note all the detective work we have done with the four lines provided. As we went through the dialogue step-by-step, what I pointed out probably seemed, on one level, rather obvious and certainly elementary. It was. On the other hand, if I had not pointed out all these obvious spots on the map, would you have noticed them? And would you have considered their primary importance to solving the acting problems contained in this four-line script? The honest answer is probably no. You might not have considered what we just did with the lines as an acting problem at all—as a problem that the actor needs to solve.

What we have done so far was not difficult. It certainly does not compare even remotely with the kind of analysis that a Sherlock Holmes might engage in. It was, in fact, much more elementary. Nevertheless, Watson, the little process we have just gone through required us to pay careful attention to the words on the page and apply to them some practical common sense. Everyone reading this page can do that. And actors must do that—if they are going to solve the riddle of the script that leads to making good choices.

The difficult part of all this, if there is a difficulty at all, lies in the way you read the printed word. As an actor you must be willing to train yourself to read actively. I noted in the first chapter that actors today tend to be aliterate. They do not like to read and do so unwillingly and unhappily when they have to. But if you look at reading a script as detective work, rather than that odious thing called "reading," you will begin to condition yourself to read actively. Reading actively means that you ask questions about the script. Finding the answers to those questions will lead you to solving the problem of the scene and the play. In other words, reading actively will lead you to the discovery of what the story is and how to play it. It will lead you to the actions that your character must execute for the story of the play to be told effectively. These selected and executed actions will, in turn, ultimately take you a long way toward effectively creating the character you play for the audience.

Now back to our four-line play and the subject of conflict. The only definite conflict we can discern occurs at the moment when it is time for the two characters to depart from each other. Since we have no other facts about these two characters and this situation, we can and must make up the other necessary details on our own. The only restrictions are that we must be able to justify the lines, and we must follow the definition of good acting—because it will serve us to do so. Remember that definition. *To be believable and to tell the best possible story while serving the script.* Since we have already sucked out all that is in the provided script, we don't need to worry about that any further. But we do need, of course, to be believable, and we do want to tell the best story we can. That means refocusing on the conflict.

The logical question is, what would cause these two characters to not want to depart from each other? The answer to that question will come through the given circumstances of the story and from the action up to this point. The given circumstances are the who, what, when, and where of the story. Who are characters involved in the action? What is it, exactly, that they are doing? When are they doing it, and where? In a normal script the playwright usually provides this information in his or her stage directions, or through implication in the script by what characters say and do. We have none of that background stuff in our four-line play, so we must provide it ourselves. We must not, however, simply provide ourselves with arbitrary answers.

Any choices we make should serve to tell the best possible story and serve the script as written. In our four-line play we could make an infinite number of choices. Infinite numbers are far harder to deal with than finite ones. The given circumstances of a fully fleshed-out play make possibilities far narrower and in some ways far easier, if we read actively. Be that as it may, in our four line play, we are obligated as actors to create the necessary details using the script and our common sense if we are going to create a story that we can consider complete.

The question again, then. What would cause our two characters to not want to depart from each other? Since a change comes after the greeting and before the "well," it seems logical that something happens between the two characters, and the thing that happens makes them want or need to stay connected. The first thing that comes to my mind is love. Since there are no wrong answers here, the next question to ask is, would having these two characters fall for each other make for a good story, and would that story be believable? The answer, I think, is yes. Could this choice be justified by the dialogue? Again, the answer is yes. Finally, can you think of a better choice—a choice that would make for a better story? If so, I leave that to you. But I can't think of one at the moment, so I am going to commit to that choice. Love, or some kind of attraction, makes these characters want to stay together.

The conflict, then, emerges because these two characters, as a result of seeing each other, want to stay together but they can't. They must move on. Why? The dialogue suggests they do. They say "See ya" and "Bye," after all. Perhaps you're thinking right now that maybe they say good-bye but don't really move on. I'm willing to accept that, but I'm not willing to say they just mutually decide not to go. That would not be interesting. That choice provides no conflict. In that scenario everything is easy, and therefore not interesting to watch or, for that matter, to act.

Keep in mind that the story becomes or remains interesting only when something is at stake. When characters take risks, the story is interesting. When characters must overcome obstacles, the story is interesting. When characters share the stage with other characters who have opposing wants and needs, the story is very interesting. So even if both characters decide to stay, something must be at risk so that there is a source of conflict. That risk must be found in the given circumstances, which in this case we as actors will have to provide ourselves.

Suppose, for instance, that A and B come from different backgrounds. A's group hates B's group. A and B are teenagers, let's say, A a boy, B a girl. This information constitutes the *who*. Suppose that A and B are out searching for food or firewood. That is the *what*. The scene takes place in the forest on the planet Z 94. That is the *where*. Suppose it is night fall in the year 2783. That is the *when*.

Note that some of the given circumstances I've offered you are more useful than others. Having the scene take place in the forest, for instance, is useful. A forest conjures up things you can do and ways to do them. The planet Z 94 is less so. Little comes to mind that I can connect with that planet that will give me things as an actor to do. And if I come up with something bizarre to do because I have decided Z 94 is a strange planet, there is no guarantee that the audience will get that. They have no frame of reference for Z 94, either. Remember, the choices we make must serve the audience as well as ourselves. The stories we tell are for them.

Nightfall is good. Vision may be unreliable, and that can provide obstacles and perhaps conflict. The year 2783 is far less useful. How will I be able to get across that this scene takes place far in the future, and does that really matter in the particular four-line play? Will setting the play in the future give me something to work with? Probably not. The point is, if we are inventing given circumstances, we want to invent circumstances that will add to the story and help make it clear.

So the given circumstances we have imposed on the lines of dialogue (reprinted here for convenience) now provide a basic scenario from which we can build a story. Compare the lines with the scenario and see if the added given circumstances can be supported and justified by the lines.

A. Hello!
B. Hi.
A. Well. See ya.
B. Yeh. Bye.

The story goes something like this:

A, a teenage boy, and B, a teenage girl from different tribes on the planet Z 94, are in the forest at nightfall, collecting food and wood. Suddenly, they stumble upon each other in a clearing. At first they don't see each other in the dimming light. Then, as they greet each other coolly, their eyes meet. Something strong ignites between them. Though each of them is obligated to return home as quickly as possible, neither wants to leave. Finally, A realizes that the two of them have been magnetized to each other, and with an awkward word or two, he breaks the spell between them and unhappily starts to take his leave. B acknowledges that she, too, has been mesmerized but agrees that they must depart. With an impulsive gesture, A moves toward B and gives her a light kiss on the cheek. As he pulls away, B grabs his hands, pulls him back to her, and kisses him far more passionately, on the lips. The two finally break away from the embrace, look at each other deeply, back away, and turn and run into the trees in separate directions.

Now, that sounds like a pretty good story, right? A bit familiar, perhaps, but one that would certainly give you plenty to act and act well in the audition you are about to perform. Though I have embellished the scenario even more than was discussed earlier, I put nothing in it that is inconsistent with the lines the playwright provided. I decided to have the characters kiss at the end of the scenario because I thought it made for a better story. It upped the stakes and added a risk factor.

The conflict, person versus person, was present at the beginning of the scene. Two enemies accidentally confronting each other would provide that conflict, but the eye contact between them changes all that, so there is already a nice arc to the story. The characters are drawn to each other, but each knows that this is not right. Their conflict then becomes internal. There is no conflict as they kiss, but the conflict returns when each discovers, as Romeo and Juliet did, that they have the desire to stay but need to go. The two vanishing into the woods after a fulfilling moment between them makes for a nice finish. Now the story has a solid beginning, middle, and end.

Notice that this description of the story both implies and states directly the actions that the actors as characters would have to carry out. These actions are as important to the telling of the story and to the revelation of character as the dialogue is. In fact, probably more so. This is an important lesson to keep in mind. Dialogue helps tell the story, but it is only one element of the storytelling machinery. What we do onstage or on screen tells the audience what we as characters are thinking and feeling and propels the story forward every bit as much as the words do.

The manner in which the described actions are carried out will further define the story and its characters. How each kiss is actually physicalized by the actors will add to the story. How each character reacts to the kiss will add to the story. Every physical detail, planned in advance or discovered in the moment, will add to the story and to the characters telling that story. This leads me to a final point.

All of the analysis work just described is part of the homework every actor must do before putting his or her work up on the stage or screen. But once actors begin to work with each other, that homework must be adjusted to accommodate the other actor's choices. The actor playing A has brought his private mental movie to the audition. The actor playing B has brought hers. All their choices must be bent in order to work within the movie being created when the two actors put their choices together to create the actual scene. If A and B have time to work together before the audition, they can smooth out their differences through the rehearsal process. If they do not have the time, then the two actors must be willing at every moment to listen to each other with all their senses. They must be willing to adjust to any new input as it develops. This will give the work the feel of happening for the first time.

Through the analysis process, we covered many of the tools described in the first chapter. We analyzed the script starting with an active reading. We found the conflict and arc of the story by discovering the cause-and-effect progression of the action. We searched for the given circumstances and added to them when necessary in ways that would justify the script and enhance it. We maximized the conflict by adding risk and obstacle to our work. We noted and developed the big moments in the unfolding story, and we acknowledged that this basic game plan can be adjusted in accordance with how it plays out moment-to-moment with a scene partner.

It should be noted, however, that in an actual script you will have to provide far fewer given circumstances solely from your imagination, because the playwright will probably provide you with much more to go on. But that means you will have to peruse that script even more closely than we did for the four-line scene if you are to find the details that will help you bring the work to life. You will need to sort through those given circumstances to find the ones that you can convert to actions—actions that are clear and compelling onstage. This part of the work will always remain a challenge that you as an actor must face each time you pick up a new script to begin your work. Hopefully, you will come to consider it a challenge that brings you great pleasure as you continue to develop your craft.

What we have not done, of course, is to develop a series of specific physical actions that will serve us in telling the story. The scenario we developed here suggests a number of those actions, but only the actual physicalization of those actions through the rehearsal process will enable us to fully bring them to life and make them work effectively. Nor have we examined the psychological actions of the scene from the viewpoint of the actors playing the characters. That means we have not specifically thought about what the characters do and what they want to gain by doing it. Again, these psychological actions and motivations have been suggested in our discussion, but these actually require a much more specific scrutiny. To use both kinds of actions effectively—like so much of what an actor must do—starts with finding the conflict at the core of any play or scene. Playing actions effectively is the most important element in telling the story of the play clearly and compellingly for an audience. We will examine this aspect of the work more closely in the next chapter.

COLLECTING THE STORY PIECES

HERE IS ANOTHER SCENE WITHOUT CONTEXT. CAN YOU determine the conflict?

> A. Wanna play?
> B. With you?
> A. No, with my mother. Come here.
> B. Wait. All right, let's play.

Initially, there is not a lot to grab on to here. But if you have been paying close attention up to this point, you'll remember that stories center on a conflict, and that it is necessary to know the context or given circumstances of the dialogue to help you determine that conflict. Again, as with our earlier four-line scene, no given circumstances are provided, so we will have to make them up. But remember, whatever we make up has to be justified and consistent with the script.

What do we know, then? We know that something is going on between A and B—they are the only two characters available to work with, so the conflict must be between them. And we know that the central issue seems to be about the matter of *playing*—first whether B will accept A's offer to play, and then whether B will adhere to A's seeming order to "come here."

Of course, the script implies that B eventually does so. But since we want to create and use conflict effectively, it is important that B go through some process of deciding both to go to A and to play. Thought of in these terms, two possible conflicts quickly emerge.

1. Person versus person — will A get B to come even if B resists?
2. Internal — will B decide to go to A and "play," or not?

Now that we have made some decisions regarding the conflict, we will need to develop the other given circumstances. Of particular importance is the *what* of the scene — just what is the "play" that B is offering A? The script does not tell us, so whatever we come up with will make up the foundation of the scene, because it will be the source of the conflict. We will also have to decide on the other given circumstances, who A and B are, when the scene takes place, and where. All of these factors will contribute to the story and how it must eventually unfold.

But for now let's just focus on the *what*. Suppose I said that the *what* of the scene is a game of pool. Once we establish that, the dialogue falls into place and we automatically start to know something about the *who*, as well. We also begin to imagine something about what the action of the scene might be like. A asks B if B wants to play some pool. B then asks for some clarification, considers the prospect of playing with A, or with A's mother, and then seems to agree. Deciding on the other given circumstances should further clarify the action of the story and help focus the many choices that remain to be made.

Using action — both physical and psychological — to tell the story was one of Konstantin Stanislavski's most important contributions to the development of acting craft. The word *action* has several meanings specific to the acting process, and even to the four-line snippet of dialogue under consideration.

Action can refer to:

- the arc or throughline of the story being told — what happens, in what order
- the sum total of what the actor as character does in a play or scene
- the things an actor chooses to do psychologically and/or physically as a character in the play, the scene, or the moment

In this chapter we will refer to all three meanings, but the third meaning will be our primary focus.

ACTION — PHYSICAL AND PSYCHOLOGICAL

In the early days of Stanislavski's search for a tangible acting technique, he believed that finding and focusing on emotional truth would enable the actor to best tell the story of the play. But later in his search, he came to believe that playing actions was far clearer and more reliable for reaching that end. He also learned that playing well-selected actions could lead to a full and truthful connection with the actor's emotions. (If I bang a table with my fist as though I were very angry, I will feel something akin to anger.) Besides, actions can be interpreted more easily by an audience, and actors can more easily access actions than emotions directly.

Two kinds of actions can and should be played by any actor, according to Stanislavski. The first kind was demonstrated in the previous chapter. These actions refer to what an actor as character literally chooses to do and then actually does. These *physical actions* are sometimes spontaneous, but are never best left to impulse alone. By choosing what to do and how to do it, the actor can tell the story effectively and demonstrate a great deal about the character being played. You will learn a lot about this subject in the next couple of chapters, but here is a quick example.

> A. Wanna play?
> B. With you?
> A. No, with my mother. Come here.
> B. Wait. All right, let's play.

PHYSICAL ACTION

Suppose that character A raises the pool stick he is holding in his hand when he says that first line. A then turns to the table, grabs the white cue ball with a free hand, places it in its opening position, and quickly hits a break shot with great velocity. At least one ball falls into a hole. A turns back toward B, smiling. B fans his or her face, then puts his or her hands on the sides of his or her cheeks and holds them there before saying the line, "With you?"

Based on the description above, what do you think B is thinking? What do you think B is feeling? Though no two audience members will necessarily agree totally about B's thoughts and feelings, most members of the audience will have drawn some conclusions after watching this series of actions. The playwright has written nothing about B's reaction to the pool shot. Therefore, all the physical-action choices, either planned or spontaneous, will need to come from the imagination of the actor playing character B rather than from the script itself.

But whether spontaneous or planned, these choices are no doubt very telling. If they came spontaneously out of the rehearsal process, the actor will have to decide whether these choices are effective and appropriate for the character and for the story at this particular time. If they are, the actor may want to further develop or modify them. If they happened on impulse in performance, whether these choices are ideal or not, the actors onstage must play off of what has occurred. Since the audience has seen this sequence happen, the actors must react to this information, as well, and make choices based on those newly introduced actions.

But the problem with spontaneous choices is that they can lead away from the story that the playwright has provided in the script. In a good script, the words and actions provided by the playwright, stated or implied, are there for a specific reason—a reason carefully thought through by that playwright. Remember, the playwright has written more lines that have yet to be spoken, and those lines must connect with the dialogue and actions that preceded them.

Some actors believe that any strong choice, heartfelt and spontaneous and coming as a genuine reaction to a moment, is valid. This kind of thinking, though, can bend, mutilate, or destroy what the playwright intended. Several of these spontaneous choices strung together by the actors onstage can take the script or their characterizations so far afield that the play will never get back on track. Is it any wonder, then, that sometimes we go to see a production of a well-received play and can't figure out why anyone would find it worthy? The intended story has been buried, the characterizations have been mutated, and the intended meaning of the play has been irrevocably changed or even destroyed. The play seems to make no sense whatsoever, though we may still admire the performances because of their believability and power.

But physical actions that have been selected specifically to forward the story of the play or film keep it on track and reveal character details that, in turn, add to what the playwright provided. Well-chosen physical actions put flesh on the bones of the blueprint we call the script, and they add colors and levels not necessarily apparent when we read the script on the printed page. The way Hannibal Lecter sniffs the air as Clarice Starling approaches his cell is every bit as powerful and frightening as anything the screenwriter gave him to say. The manner in which Hannibal tilts his head when he looks at Clarice can raise goose bumps on the dead. That sucking sound that Anthony Hopkins as Lecter chose to make when describing something delicious will be imitated for generations. Some, if not all, of these actions came from the actor, not the script. These choices forward the story and add dimension to the character. Obviously, these choices came from the mind and imagination of a thoughtful actor using more than his instincts.

All this is not to say that there is no place for spontaneous, in-the-moment choices or the use of instinct. There is. But only a small percentage of actors can truly rely on their instincts alone to produce actions that propel the story forward compellingly and reliably. Craft is about having a set of tools on which you can depend. There is nothing wrong with exploring with instinct and being in the moment, but the choices that develop from this approach must be examined, edited, and refined if they are going to amount to more than self-indulgence at the expense of the script.

PSYCHOLOGICAL ACTION

Psychological action refers to what the actor as character is trying to accomplish at every moment of his or her stage or film time. This kind of action is more often referred to as an *objective* or *intention*. It can also be called an *action, goal, need,* or *want.* But no matter what you name it, as an actor you must be playing one of these at all times during your stage life.

Adhering to this rule — the playing of an objective at all times — creates one of the biggest differences between real life and what an actor does onstage. We spend much of our real-life time doing and saying things spontaneously as we react to the moment-by-moment progression of the day. We seldom give our words and actions much introspection. Too often, only as we push our shoes off at the end of the day do we replay and think about the movie of our lives that has played out for the previous eighteen hours. We may at that time say to ourselves, "Why the hell did I do that to Roger?" or, "What was I thinking when I spoke to Janet that way?" We may even get introspective and come up with a reason or two. But most of our moment-to-moment transactions in real life are reactive and spontaneous, at least on a conscious level. They are seldom part of a specific game plan.

This should not be the case when we are acting. Our acting choices should be part of a game plan. When it is done well, acting often seems like real life, but it differs. As an actor you must play out a series of actions that correspond and support the story you are telling. Not just any choice will do. Only choices that serve the script by forwarding the story and making clear the thoughts and feelings of the character you are playing will serve. Though your objectives may change during the course of the play as circumstances cause them to, you will never be without the need to be play a single objective specifically.

Remember, the playwright or screenwriter has set down the railroad tracks of the story, and your choices must keep the story on track. In life you have no such obligation. What happens next is not necessarily part of your plan — because you can't read ahead in the story of your life. But when living a life onstage, you can and must read ahead. Yes, all of the choices you carry out must seem like they are happening for the first time here and now, as if they are new. But that is the illusion you create as an actor. The fact is you have read all the pages that follow the moment you are in, and your choices in the moment must lead to the next as prescribed by the script.

That means that in some ways your life onstage is simpler than the one you actually live. Your range of choices is narrower, and those choices are always made purposefully. As an actor playing your character, you must make the choices intended to get you what you need — always. The script will ultimately determine whether you get what you need or not, but as the actor playing the character you must try to fulfill your need at every moment — in spite of whether the script allows you to achieve your objectives.

Why is this so related to your responsibility for telling the story? Remember the C word? *Conflict* — the engine of drama. Since the playwright has built his or her story on some kind of conflict, you must assume that whenever you are onstage, you are somehow part of that conflict, because you are part of that story. Once you identify the conflict, you can determine your part in it. What you determine should result in an action, need, want, or objective that you can play. This objective will conflict with another character's objective, usually the one sharing the stage with you, and magically, the center of the story will be created and maintained.

Now take another look at that four-line scene that began this discussion.

A. Wanna play?
B. With you?
A. No, with my mother. Come here.
B. Wait. All right, let's play.

Suppose the conflict of this scene centers on who is the better pool player, but the players themselves aren't sure. Let's say both are pool sharks, but B is not on home turf. A is. Since A has the home-court advantage, his or her objective is to first get B to play, and second beat B in the big game. There is strategy involved in this. At first A may want to intimidate B with his or her pool skills. Or A may choose to shame a hesitant B into playing by showing off. The smaller objectives you choose to play are sometimes called *tactics*. These are strategies you use to attain your overall objective—in this case, to win the pool game.

Ultimately, B also wants to win, and once B commits to playing he or she will also have to develop a strategy or a set of tactics for doing so. B's initial tactics, then, might be to demonstrate to A that A's skills do not intimidate him or her and to establish his or her own superiority.

If this is the case, how might A and B carry out the physical actions already described earlier? Would B carry out the described actions differently if truly awed by the ability A initially shows? Probably not. If B's objective is to not let A intimidate him, B would have to carry out the actions in accordance with his or her objective, even if B now realizes that he is the weaker player. Perhaps the actor can reveal a transitional moment of doubt, but if the objective is to establish his or her superiority, that is what the actor must do.

On the other hand, if B's objective were to make A like him or her rather than to establish superiority, then showing awe at A's shot might help achieve that goal. How can the actor playing B decide what action to play? That depends on knowing the playwright's entire story and what happens in the overall arc that the playwright has set down.

In this four-line scene, unless we completely determine the given circumstances, we will be unable to know the entire story. However, from the lines, we do know that B agrees to play. That means we know that whether the character feels intimidated or not, to some extent, he or she is not going to allow that feeling to stand in the way. We know that any internal conflict—whether to play or not—has been overcome. We also know that the original challenge and conflict between the two characters has been met. So that in itself is a story and certainly gives you as actors enough to play. Keep in mind that your job as the actor is to find and tell the story—the story of the play, the story of the scene, and even the story of the moment. Yes, even moments have beginnings, middles, and ends.

Once you come to understand any story and its core conflict, you will learn how to find your character's objective. It is then simply a matter of playing it and playing it fully. Playing only an action might seem simplistic. You may think that if you do only this, your work will be one-dimensional or boring. But the fact is that an audience takes in the entire story and sees your actions in terms of the bigger picture that the playwright has created. The audience comes to know and understand your character through what you do as well as through what you say. They also learn about you through what other characters say about you. By sticking to your chosen objectives, you help the story get told, and much of the complexity of your character will make it into what the audience perceives, regardless of how prosaic it may seem to you from the inside.

Please note that although you as an actor must select and play an objective for your character at all times, your character is not necessarily aware of that objective. This is the tricky part. As actors working on a role, we exist on two levels. Ultimately, some of us try to inhabit the characters we are playing, but we must never forget that we continue to be actors making choices to tell the story. If we allow ourselves to do just anything as the characters we are playing, the story will quickly lose its shape and direction. Therefore, we are obligated to make only choices for our characters that maintain the story. By choosing to play our characters' needs, we keep the story on course, because playing those objectives ensures that the conflict will be maintained and the plot forwarded.

For some fine examples of playing objectives, just check out the work of Meryl Streep, Robert De Niro, and Jack Nicholson, three of our finest film actors. Just about any of their films will do, but easy to find will be Streep in the recent *The Hours* or *The Devil Wears Prada*, De Niro in *Cape Fear* or *Taxi Driver,* and Nicholson in *The Shining* or *About Schmidt.* In each of these performances you will encounter case studies in finding strong and clear objectives to play, and staying on them. You will see complex, well-rounded characters, yet the clarity of what each of them is thinking and feeling will be both a marvel and an inspiration.

At first the idea of finding an objective to play may seem daunting. If it does, try thinking of an objective in terms of a strong verb. Under no circumstances is the verb "to be" strong. You cannot play a state of being—an *is*—and effectively tell the story. Being sad doesn't take you anywhere. Being angry doesn't take you anywhere. But asking yourself what you *do* when you're sad or angry does. You can always play actions—psychological and physical.

What do you want from the other character onstage when you feel sad? To make him cheer you up? To make him compliment you? To make him share your pain? What will you do to get what you want? Flatter him? Tickle him? Make him feel sad, too? How badly do you need what you want? How far are you willing to go to get it? These kinds of questions will lead you to your objectives, to your physical actions, and to the creation of your character.

It might help you to break down the idea of objectives into categories to make the process seem more manageable. An acting teacher I once had suggested six possible broad categories of objectives. I don't think this is by any means the only way to divide up your objective possibilities, but since I first heard the list, I have found those categories useful for my personal selection process. Thinking in terms of categories helps narrow your field of possibilities and makes them more manageable. Feel free to adapt the listed categories to your personal needs:

To give information

To get information

To make someone do something

To keep someone from doing something

To make someone feel good

To make someone feel bad

Notice that all six objectives are connected to a receiver—someone on the other end of the objective. In the first two objectives, these receivers are implied. You've got to give information to or get information from someone.

In the remaining four, the receiver is a stated part of the transaction. Any objective that you choose to play should have such a receiver. Keep in mind that your objective comes out of some conflict, so your objective should be connected to another character to ensure that the created conflict is played out with whoever shares the stage or screen with you.

Of the six objectives just listed, which do you think is the weakest—the one that gives you the least to do and, by its nature, is the least dramatic? To make someone do something, or to keep someone from doing something, implies coercion, a factor that automatically conjures conflict. To make someone feel good or bad also implies resistance and suggests an emotion at the end of the transaction. Certainly, this suggests some dramatic potential. To get information also implies some resistance, or the necessity of making someone give that information to you.

Of the six, then, to give someone information is the least dramatically fraught. Simply by giving it, the objective is accomplished. Therefore, that objective should be avoided if other possibilities exist. Only when the receiver of the information is likely to be moved by what is delivered does such an objective give the actor a strong action to play. The messengers in a Greek tragedy, for instance, can play "to give information" because the message they deliver is invariable filled with blood, gore, and terrible news; and the conflict and stakes emerge as a result of the fact that the delivering the message can put the messenger in a dangerous position.

Keep in mind that the six objectives are broad categories only. Use them only to get you started when you are stuck. Even a weak objective like "giving information" can be further refined to make it specific. That Greek messenger, for instance, might want to "make the King see what he saw" or "feel what he felt." The possibilities are endless.

You are now armed with an understanding of the two kinds of actions—physical and psychological—and you know that in any acting situation you must tell the story provided in the script by first determining the conflict and analyzing the given circumstances. We already know that our four-line scene has at least two conflicts to develop, and we now have an understanding of the arc of the story based on the *what* being a pool game. Let's take another look at the lines.

A. Wanna play?
B. With you?

A. No, with my mother. Come here.

B. Wait. All right, let's play.

We still have not discussed some elements of the story suggested by the lines. For instance, does A really suggest that B should play with his mother? And where is the "here" that A wants B to come to? And why does B say "wait" and shortly thereafter is ready to play? All of these questions must be answered and justified.

Let's continue with our already established *what*—that the given circumstances center around a pool game that seems to be important to the characters. Is it likely that A really intends for B to play A's mother? Yes, it could be possible, but the simplest strong choice would be that A is using sarcasm to help with his intimidation objective. To use sarcasm would be a *positive choice*—a choice that helps A get what he needs. Actors should always make positive choices, even if in life we do not always do so. If a choice does not help us get what our characters need, then it should not be made. Positive choices keep the conflict strong and the actor on track.

Why does B say "Wait," followed by a line that indicates he is now ready. Simple logic suggests that he did something to make himself ready. What is that action? Actor's choice. Suppose he pulls out his own pool stick and chalks it up? Or carefully puts powder on his hands in preparation for play? Either would show that he, too, has come ready to play. This sequence of actions works in terms of telling the story physically and is consistent with B's stated objective—to make A know that he or she can't be intimated, or to make A feel intimidated.

That is just one of many possibilities. B might have said "Wait" in order to give himself a moment to decide to play, if he did have an internal conflict about playing, and following the line "Wait" B could be convincing him- or herself to take the challenge. There is no right or wrong answer—only the best means to tell a compelling story consistent with the provided dialogue.

Challenge yourself to come up with other scenarios using the pool situation. Make sure that for each scenario you play a strong objective that comes from a conflict between you and the other character. Your objective's completion should be connected with your acting partner. Play your objective positively at all times, and create a throughline that is justified by the lines and tells the best story you can come up with. Use the basic six objectives listed earlier for help if you cannot think of an objective to play on your own. Remember that starting your objective with "To make the other character _____" will keep the objective strong and connected with the conflict of the scene and with your acting partner.

Once you have tried out variations of the script by making adjustments in the given circumstances and you've discovered the multitude of possibilities, you could take the script several steps further by completely changing the four W's. Suppose, for instance, that the characters were young children. Or suppose the game was Russian roulette rather than pool. Or Monopoly. Or jacks. Manipulate all the given circumstances or a few; each change will produce a new story—one that requires total adjustments concerning how you can and must play out the scene. In an actual script, many of the choices will already be provided, and it will then become your job to make sure that you see them in the script and find ways of employing them effectively. You will have done so if you tell a clear, exciting story that serves the script the story is drawn from.

CHAPTER

FIVE

SIFTING
FOR CHARACTER

WATCHING GREAT CHARACTER ACTORS LIKE DANIEL DAY-LEWIS or Robert Duvall transform themselves from role to role so that they are barely recognizable, yet totally believable, can be a thrilling experience. For many of us who know a little bit about acting, this kind of work takes the top tier in the acting pantheon. Not only are actors such as these believable and clear in their work, but who they are as personalities in their own right completely disappears within the physical transformations they seem to undergo. Anyone who has followed Daniel Day-Lewis from part to part can't help but marvel at his chameleon-like changes. From Christy Brown in *My Left Foot*, to Hawkeye in *The Last of the Mohicans*, to John Proctor in *The Crucible*, to Daniel Plainview in *There Will Be Blood*. It's hard to believe that this is the same actor. In every case, the most notable changes are the ways a character actor transforms physically and vocally. But once the looks and voice changes are noted, the things the actor chooses to do and the manner in which he does them really define a character for an audience, and ultimately this aspect of any performance becomes its most important element.

For that reason, thinking in terms of "inhabiting the character" before you can play your character's actions can be very dangerous, if not impossible. Even many fine actors never fully attain the goal of fully transforming into and inhabiting a character, and others experience it only intermittently. Yet that does not keep them from being fine actors. Young actors often operate under the misconception that they must literally become a character to do a role well. But, as with the playing of emotion, your primary purpose as an actor is to make the audience believe you are the character, whether or not you fully believe. The test lies ultimately with the audience, not with the actor.

Still, many young actors assume that total transformation is what good acting is all about. How often do I hear young actors talking about their characters as though they were some tangible entity hanging in the closet, waiting to be put on? And how seldom do I hear young actors talking about the actions of their characters and their purpose in revealing the story of the play? Yet, for the most part, the actions actors choose to play and the manner in which they carry out those chosen actions communicate character to an audience. By *action* I mean both physical and psychological—the former, what you choose to do physically; the latter, what you choose to pursue as goals during your stage time.

Playing actions will suggest character as well as give you something specific to do in a scene. Because of your chosen actions, certain character traits will seem to develop without any attempt at becoming a character. And that is 90 percent of the character game.

Of course, the other 10 percent of character is communicated to an audience through costume and other externals, like how your character moves and speaks and looks. But looking like, speaking like, and moving like a character cannot guarantee that the audience will understand the character or his or her purpose within the play's framework. In spite of this fact, many untrained actors put all their efforts into the 10 percent and allow the other 90 percent to happen by chance, inspiration, or as a result of repetition.

Character is most effectively and reliably displayed through a careful selection and execution of actions, not by magically inhabiting a character through some internal or emotional process.

I use a particular exercise with my own beginning actors at the beginning of the semester to demonstrate the points I am making here. The game, called Character Roll Call, goes something like this.

I start by asking my students to answer, "Here," when I call their name. I tell them to answer as themselves as though attendance were actually being taken. I ask the class to observe each other very carefully during the process and to make determinations about each class member based on what they see and hear. They may even take notes if they want to in order to better help them remember what they observed.

After the first round is played, I have my students report on what they observed. Essentially, they draw conclusions from their limited first impressions—based simply on what they saw and heard as each student had his or her brief moment in the spotlight. Most of the time, the majority of the class will report on the same few students. These students end up as the featured subjects because they did something noteworthy when it was their turn to say "Here." The rest of the class was quickly forgotten in the discussion. It may have been a gesture that made particular individuals stand out, or the way the scripted word was uttered, or it may have been something in the exchange that went on between me as the teacher and those individuals as the students.

If a particular student was singled out as a result of the fact that she drew attention in an unbelievable way—in a way that would not be accepted in an actual classroom setting—it was either noted by the class or I would point it out myself. An example of this kind of choice might be if an actor, when it is her turn to say "here," jumped from her seat and screamed it at the top of her lungs, or if a student made an obscene gesture to note his presence. This kind of choice would certainly be memorable, but at the expense of having the exercise equally balanced for each member of the class. But more importantly, this kind of choice would not be believable, and believability is always part of the three-pronged definition of good acting. The purpose of the exercise is, after all, to create a fully believable acting situation, not to get a laugh or draw attention for its own sake.

After general comments have been made, I ask the class what they learned about each other in terms of who they really are—based what was observed. In acting terms, this is a reference to character. This question usually proves to be a tough one. Usually very few conclusions are drawn, because each student's response to the roll call was intended only to inform me that he or she was present. They did not attempt to convey more information than this, and anything more that the class observed would not have resulted from any particular choice being made. Usually any conclusions drawn by the class would turn out to be inaccurate, since there was no purpose behind the action—vocal and physical—that the individuals in the class took on.

As a result of the group discussion, my class will usually conclude that any demonstration of character under the circumstances of the first round of the exercise was sketchy at best. They had too little time and too little opportunity to inhabit and communicate character. Of course, as the exercise points out, there was also no direct attempt to establish character—in spite of the fact that each of my students was the character he or she was playing. Obviously, then it takes more than being a character to communicate character. And that is the point. Simply inhabiting character does not necessarily communicate character.

In the second round of the exercise, I ask my students to think of a dominant personality characteristic they possess. It could be anything from shyness to egotism to a great sense of humor to sadness or cynicism. Once they have pinpointed this characteristic, I ask them to come up with a single physical action demonstrating this quality that they could believably execute when their name is called during the next round of attendance taking. The key here is twofold. First, they will have to come up with an action that actually suggests the quality, which, depending on the characteristic, could be difficult indeed. If they can't come up with an action to represent the characteristic, I tell them to change the quality they are trying to communicate. The idea in acting is to always make choices that can be carried out successfully.

The second task, I remind them, is to keep in mind they must be "believable" at all times. Whatever actions they select to perform, these actions must fit in believably during the roll taking. A chosen action must seem natural. It must also respect the balance of the overall exercise. It other words, an individual's chosen action must not cause an untoward shift that makes the exercise about them at the expense of the rest of the class. I always take the roll in real time, so the individual moments each actor has in the spotlight must take no more than real time would allow.

In this round of the game, my actors have a much larger body of work to discuss. Because everyone in the class had to make choices, chances are even if not every choice was absolutely clear, far more of them were interesting, because thought went into their selection. Further, more students willingly guessed at the personality characteristics suggested through the actions presented, because this time through they were more than random and spontaneous reactions of the moment. In other words, because of the specific choices of action, character emerged. And the point of all this is that the exercise is not unlike any scripted acting situation in which an actor has the obligation to be believable, serve the overall script, and do the things his or her character would do under the circumstances while forwarding their own storytelling responsibilities. Each of the actors in the exercise in round two were responsible for the following:

- executing actions that seemed real rather than acted
- executing actions that came naturally out of the situation
- saying "Here" in a way that was consistent with the actions being played and reflecting the ongoing progression in the scene

They also needed to accomplish the following:

- making and executing choices that led to a natural flow from one student to the next
- listening and reacting even when it wasn't their turn to perform in the spotlight, and listening in a way consistent with who they are in real life, since they were playing the character of themselves
- making their time in the spotlight reflective of their personality trait without any extra mustard
- making their moments in real time and without commenting on their work

A central point of the ensemble element of this game is that an actor must maintain the action of his or her character even when not in principal focus. In life, no one stops being who they are when they are not speaking, yet so often, beginning actors think they are acting only when they have lines. Childish, no? Each time you respond as a character, execute an action, carry out some business, or move toward or away from someone or something, you add to the audience's perception of your character. In fact, the sum total of all the actions you execute create for the audience the illusion of character. The audience will put together the kindness you show in one scene, the anger demonstrated in another, and the intelligence or whimsicality of other moments and mix all the pieces into a complex whole, just the way people do in life. If you come alive only for your spoken moments, you can never expect to be fully believed or to produce a fully realized character.

In the third round of Roll Call, I ask my students to take a moment and come up with a strong personality trait that they can translate into a physical action or series of actions. My actors are now free from the strictures of trying to portray themselves truthfully. They are now free to step outside of themselves and be more creative.

Since my students have now been freed from any introspective self-analysis and the self-consciousness that could come from having to expose any personal characteristics, a much wider range of characters responds to my attendance taking. Sometimes in this round I even tell my students that they must portray first graders, or sixth graders, or college students. And if I'm feeling really brave, I might tell them that they must become seniors in a remedial class or students in an ESL class. The basic rules of the exercise still apply, but my students now have to adapt their playable characteristic to the specific circumstances dictated.

In another variation of the game I ask my students to go to the board and write their names after they say "Here." In this case, what they do and how they do it can be defined even more elaborately. Included in their acting responsibilities are such things as:

- reacting to their name as they are called
- getting up and moving to the board
- writing on the board
- returning to their seats

Whenever I do this round of the exercise, students always feel a tremendous temptation to "act" or to get a laugh at the expense of making the actions believable and clearly executed. Beginning actors like to perform, but most of the time when you come from performance mode you're doing it at the expense of believability You've got to make choices that characters would actually do in the given circumstances.

The way people move, their tempo when they move, how quickly they react to their name being called, whether they look at the teacher when they move toward the board, whether they look at their classmates as they move to the board, how they write their name, and the manner in which they return to their seats will profoundly affect how they are perceived. Each of the elements making up your total physical actions will tell the audience something accurate or misleading, depending on the quality of your choices and their execution. For that reason, you must think through what you will do before attempting to do it in front of an audience.

Sometimes I ask my students to write down a short character description (a paragraph or so) before attempting the exercise. Then I ask them to actually write down what they will do when they present their Roll Call contribution in class. The choices they make should amplify in a tangible way the attributes they described in their paragraph. Otherwise, the writing assignment would be a wasted effort. I then give them time to rehearse what they have written down. The paragraph and the selected choices should serve as a guide to their rehearsal process. If, however, while in the process of rehearsing they make discoveries that would alter their character description or their written selected actions, I make them update the written material to reflect the final version they will present in class. Sticking to a game plan is a good habit for you to learn. It is part of the discipline that a good actor must master. Then I let them perform their work. Most of the time, the well-thought-out and rehearsed work will be clearer, more interesting, and more believable than the work created on the spot. The reasons by this point should be clear.

By the end of this sequence of exercises, my students are pretty well convinced that character can be created through a series of actions without the need to somehow completely transform themselves into the character being played. They also understand that successful acting usually results from careful analysis and planning rather than from simply relying on intuition and spontaneous brilliance. Of course, the acting process reserves a special place for those who can live in the moment and react, but most actors cannot afford to rely on that ability alone.

Though Roll Call primarily focuses on communicating the concept of character through action, it might also imply, incorrectly, that actors should go onstage and simply play character choices and ignore the more important obligation to make choices that will help tell the story of the play. You should at all times play actions that help you obtain your acting objectives (or psychological actions). When you do so, you will meet your obligation to get the story across, as well as create character. Ultimately, the actor as character must not only say "Here" and walk to the board and write his name; he must also fulfill some need of the character, whether the character is aware of it or not. In turn, playing this psychological action helps reveal character and forwards the story.

Remember that this exercise is intended to get actors to use the given circumstances effectively and to realize the importance of making specific choices—choices that will tell the story of the scene and reveal who you are through what you do. These choices can come only as a result of fully understanding and using the circumstance of the situation and by being very clear about what you as actor/characters are trying to do in that situation.

In other words, you must have a specific purpose to play out, based on the selected situation, and make choices that will attempt to fulfill that purpose or objective.

Too often, actors tend to go to the dialogue without fully understanding and using the context in which the dialogue is delivered. The more specific you are about the given circumstances, the more your work can be carried out in a specific and clear manner. Stories that actors choose to tell should be as compelling as possible, but the situations laid out in the Roll Call exercise make that automatic. However, when actors fail to lay out for themselves all elements of the given circumstances — the who, what, when, and where of the situation they select — their work is likely to be little more than generalized and superficial. In addition, when actors fail to have a specific objective when playing out the chosen situation, their selected actions will probably fail to create a well-told story or demonstrate character.

The elements of craft can be developed and mastered regardless of talent. Therefore, the outside-in approach to the creation of character can and will work for you. For the less naturally gifted, using an analysis and choice-making process can lead to success despite a lack of intuitive ability for creating character. For those few who are extremely gifted, approaching the creation of character through craft will enable you to harness your gifts reliably and consistently, and will give you the tools to make good choices even during those times when talent and intuition do not work to capacity. Whether you go from the outside in or from the inside out, the bottom line is always what the audience gets from the work. If your character is revealed and if the story is well told, the work has been successful, with or without full inhabitation.

Each of the exercises described here were based on the premise that character arises more from playing appropriate actions than from actually inhabiting the inner world of a particular character. That is not to say that when an actor merges with the character he or she is playing, it is not a wonderful thing. It is, and for those actors who have such an experience it can be gratifying for them, as well as for the audience watching. But to suggest that "becoming the character" is the proper way to approach the playing of one would probably prove to be frustrating and, for many of you, impossible.

In summary, then, character can be established and made clear to an audience through the playing of actions — psychological and physical — based on an analysis of the playwright's script. What an actor as character does onstage is far more revealing and dependable than any attempt to magically inhabit that character. It is more revealing because as actors we can select the specific actions our characters will execute, and, by a systematic analysis of the play and a careful selection process, those actions can tell the audience precisely what they need to know about the unfolding story and about the individual carrying out those actions. This approach is more dependable than an internal approach, because the playing of actions is, by its nature, doable. The playing of actions does not rely on emotions that may come and go — or that may not be conjurable at all. An audience can see an action and make judgments based on what they see. Even when an actor generates emotion organically, the audience may not see what the actor feels, or they may interpret what they see as what that actor is feeling. Nor will the playing of spontaneous emotion necessarily lead an actor to a series of choices that will support the story the playwright has set out to tell. Playing emotion is simply not dependable, but playing action is.

When Jack Nicholson as the lonely widower in *About Schmidt* leans in to kiss his attractive and married next-door neighbor in the kitchen of her mobile home, there is no doubt about what he is trying to do and what he is thinking and feeling. We know as a result of what we have already learned about him during the unfolding story, and from what he has chosen to do and the manner in which he carries it out. Nicholson's slow and tender incline toward his attractive neighbor is awkward and unsure. It demonstrates character. The rejection he soon meets with is both funny (to us in the audience) and surprising, and his ignominious departure is clumsy, embarrassing, and poignant. We see all this as a result of what he does. There is no dialogue to help us get what Schmidt is feeling.

All of the actions carried out by Nicholson may have been a spontaneous reaction that resulted from inhabiting his character, but after following Nicholson's body of work for so many years, to draw that conclusion would probably be short-changing this master film actor. Jack Nicholson has far too many savvy portrayals under his belt to imply that instinct alone makes his performances so reliably clear and effective. His range of performances, from *One Flew over the Cuckoo's Nest* to *A Few Good Men* to *As Good as It Gets,* makes that point all too convincingly. All of Nicholson's portrayals offer selected actions that give us what we need to know about the story and about his character. Often these selected actions are memorable as well as revealing and specific. Nicholson is clearly an actor who thinks about what he will do in a scene—in terms of both psychological and physical actions.

The Nicholson example summarizes the points made in the exercises offered up in previous chapters, but it also suggests that there is more to this character stuff than the playing of actions alone. I have avoided discussing some other aspects of playing character until now because I did not want to put the horse before the cart. These aspects are often referred to as the *externals* of character. They include the following:

1. Physical adjustments—voice, speech, posture, manner of movement

2. Outward trappings—costume, makeup

3. Physical states—such as drunkenness, sickness, depression, elation

I selected Jack Nicholson as an example for this chapter for a specific reason beyond the fact that I admire his work. Nicholson is often considered a personality actor because of the strength of his own personality, which clearly comes through in all of his performances. But Nicholson is a character actor, as well, and has often made physical choices that go far beyond his own natural inclinations and that, as a result, demonstrate clearly the character he is playing (*About Schmidt, Hoffa, Batman, As Good as It Gets*). He has also embraced costumes and makeup as an integral part his body of work and has effectively used both to enhance his performances (*Hoffa, Wolf, Batman, As Good as It Gets*). Finally, he is no stranger to playing physical states such as drunkenness, depression, or sexual arousal (*Terms of Endearment, Reds, Carnal Knowledge,* and *The Postman Always Rings Twice*). But his performances rarely become about playing these qualities at the expense of his more important obligation to tell the story—a pitfall that many actors, particularly young ones, are unable to avoid falling into. Even when his characters are drunk, depressed, or aroused, they manage to pursue objectives and play actions that forward the story with clarity.

Inspired by the Nicholson model is an exercise that employs all the elements of character work but, unlike the exercises in Roll Call, is connected to the script and the need for actors to make choices that serve it.

Select a character from a play you have read and begin to create a one-person scene for that character, a scene suggested by the play but not actually in it. The scene may include a few lines of dialogue that you will make up. The dialogue must be consistent with and justified by the circumstances of the scene created and consistent with your character. Once you have decided on a character and a scene, develop the scene moment by moment, first by writing it out, and then by rehearsing it. When you are finished rehearsing, you can play it for your class if you are currently in one, or for some actor friends for feedback.

The idea is to write a detailed description of your chosen character that will include physical, intellectual, and emotional elements. The description might consist of a written paragraph or a thought-out list of adjectives that describe the character. For each described quality or chosen adjective there should be a written justification. Your justification can include pieces of dialogue from the play that support the inclusion of that characteristic, described actions that support its inclusion, or stage direction that supports it. When completed, you can use this descriptive analysis as the source for your character synthesis.

You should also write a scenario that describes the scene you will eventually present. Included in the scenario should be the central conflict for your character, the character's objective in the scene, and a description of the step-by-step action or arc of the scene. Clearly identify the scene's beginning, middle, and end in the paragraph. Your scenario should be specific, because it will eventually be turned into your actual physical-action score.

Once your score is completed, you are ready to develop your character scene.

Now you will develop the step-by-step physical action of the scene distilled from the conflict of the scene and your character's objective, as well as a particular manner of movement and speech consistent with the character. You will select costumes and personal props that help tell the story of the scene and reveal the specifics of your character.

Once you put it all together and rehearse it, you're ready to show it to an audience for feedback. You will probably have learned a lot along the way.

This difficult exercise includes many elements that have been touched on in the earlier character exercises. But it also includes elements not previously worked on. The voice and movement obligation, for instance, is new terrain and could easily become over-the-top or lead you into indicating rather than organic acting. But going through the experience of thinking in terms of making vocal and movement choices consistent with the character you are playing is worth the risk. Since each of the choices you ultimately make will have to be justified in writing, you choices will need to be well thought out, even if they are not perfectly performed. Hopefully, you will have a chance to get feedback, which, of course is the best way to find out if you are doing too much. Feedback will give you the chance to begin formulating parameters for what works and what doesn't.

The assignment as presented here is a one-person scene, but you could easily adapt the principal elements of the exercise to a two-character scene with actual dialogue. I have chosen this format because it allows you to work alone without the problems attendant when you have to find someone else to work with. But if the scene-study format works better for you, by all means, proceed in that manner.

And now some notes on the exercise. Putting into writing the work you are going to do ensures that your thought process has actually been completed. Too often, actors formulate a fuzzy idea of what they think or what they are going to do, and fuzzy thought usually leads to fuzzy action. Besides, a written character description, and a written description of the action of the scene including all actions to be played, will give you a specific road map to use on your journey. It will also serve as a tangible reminder that what you are doing always comes from choices. These choices should be specific, but they may be changed if and when you discover that they don't work or because you make new discoveries about the scene and character as the rehearsal process progresses.

What follows is a partial character description that you can use as a sample. It is for Laura from *The Glass Menagerie,* a play that is probably familiar to you. For each item listed in the character description, there is a justification from the script. This should be an important part of your process, because it ensures that you use your script carefully and practically. Note that any description defining a quality of the character will have to be translated into a playable action in the next part of step one.

The three most obvious characteristics of Laura are her shyness, her inferiority complex, and the fact that she is partially crippled. We know that she is shy because it is mentioned by each of the characters at some point, but it is especially obvious during her scene with the gentleman caller, who comments on it, and during the yearbook scene when she talks to her mother about her shyness in a class with Jim. The fact that one of her legs is shorter than the other is part of the description that the playwright gives us, and it is a big factor in the development of her other dominant qualities — that shyness and that feeling of inferiority. Laura describes her self-consciousness about her leg when she tells Jim how her walking thundered when she entered singing class late and everyone could see and hear her as she entered. Jim concludes that Laura has an inferiority complex and tells her so in their scene together.

Obviously, Laura's crippledness is a physical characteristic and can be played directly. But how crippled is she? This will factor into the character work developed. If walking is difficult, then her reasons for self-consciousness are obvious and her reasons to feel inferior overtly understandable. But if her limp is small, it tells us something else about her character — that she has allowed a smaller issue to overcome her potential. Which choice is better for the story, and why? You would need to justify and support your answer and use the physicality in your presented scene.

Shyness is a quality that cannot be played directly, but the manner in which Laura carries out all of her actions can suggest shyness. You will have to decide how a shy person might carry out actions in a manner distinct from the way a confident person might. You might want to study the actions of a shy person you actually know, or you will need to recall times in which you have felt shy and think very specifically about how you behaved at those times.

Now here is a sample description of the scene that the actor playing Laura might come up with:

The scene I have invented would occur after the actual play has ended. Jim has announced that he is already engaged, and has left only a few minutes ago. Tom and Amanda have argued bitterly, and he has left, never to return. Amanda is in her room crying, and Laura returns to the living room to make herself feel less alone by playing with her glass menagerie. The conflict in the scene is that she hears her mother crying, and part of her wants to go to her mother, but the other part of her needs to escape the reality of the fact that her one chance for happiness and normality has now vanished. She is afraid her mother is angry with her as well as with Tom, and she can't face her mother's feelings. She is torn between going to her and staying. She decides to play with her animals because she must make herself feel better. That is her objective. In the story of the scene she first goes to her animals and plays a bit but then is pulled by her mother's crying and stops to listen. That is the beginning. Then she chooses to play again, and as she does, she singles out one of her little animals and continues playing. She is interrupted again by her mother's crying and stops to listen. Then she returns to her animal, looks at it closely, and gently breaks one of its legs. The audience can see now that it is a little lamb. That is the middle of the story. From that point on, Laura plays exclusively with the lamb and totally ignores her mother's crying. That is the end.

The scenario as just described has a clear conflict, an objective to play, and a story arc with a beginning, middle, and end. The scene follows logically from the given circumstances of the play, and Laura has an arc of action consistent with her established personality yet shows a justified dramatic change in herself. The fact that her mother is crying will give her a strong internal conflict to work through and should provide a platform for a very interesting scene, since a good conflict is the engine of drama. You will want to come up with a scenario that contains a strong conflict, because when you do, your acting invariably becomes much easier to execute.

During your rehearsal process, you will not only have to come up with the step-by-step sequence of actions for your character, but you will also have to set up your set, choose your costumes and props, and find ways of showing your character specifically through the manner in which you carry out your selected actions. All of these elements must be given proper thought and care. Deciding to put the menagerie upstage left simply because that's where you put it the first time you rehearsed is not an acceptable way of working. Everything an actor does should come from a choice that has purpose. This, ultimately, is what makes an artist.

In the scenario I invented, much about Laura's character will be revealed simply through what she does—playing with her animals, choosing the lamb, breaking its leg, listening to but ultimately ignoring her mother's crying. All of these actions speak loudly about who she is. As an actor, by making these choices for my scene, I have already gone a long way in creating my character, and I believe I have demonstrated my understanding that much of character comes from playing actions specifically while telling a good story. When you write your scenario, this is the point that you will most want to be thinking about.

I will not write out a complete action score here, because that territory was well covered in earlier chapters. Note, however, that my scenario strongly suggests the actions of the scene and will be easy to translate into a score. Simplicity onstage is always good. It leads to clear, understandable actions that in turn lead to clear storytelling. Do keep in mind that only the specific physical actions that the character will execute should appear on your scores. There should be no emotional adjectives or references to facial expressions that suggest such (i.e., "looks happy"). The manner in which the actions are carried out will be demonstrated in your presentations but need not appear on the action score.

The important thing is that each single action be specific, clear, and doable, and these actions should appear as part of a sequence that makes logical dramatic sense. What is written should be done without ad lib, if possible. Spontaneous add-ons are likely to take away from the logical dramatic progression that the rehearsal process should have developed. My line of dialogue, by the way, will come right at the climax of the scene when Laura decides to break her little lamb's leg. Laura will simply say, "Come here, little lamb." The manner in which she does so, as with all dialogue, will tell the underlying story here, but only the dialogue need be written on the score.

And now a note or two on costumes and props. Too often in my own classes, I see actors who pay little attention to what they wear and to what they use as props onstage. Yet I know that through my own years of experience as an actor, and my years watching other actors, that the proper selection and use of costumes and props can make all the difference in telling the story effectively and in making the character come alive. How often have I watched students playing sophisticated women present a scene in class while wearing sneakers and jeans? And how often have I seen the work completely change for the better when the dress and high heels go on? And how often have I discovered the solution to my character's physicality while rehearsing a play only after I have been given my character's costume?

The believability of a scene can be shattered because actors have not figured out when and how to smoke, or take a sip of tea, or take a bite of food. No two characters will smoke alike, drink alike, or eat alike. The way a character does each of these things tells us so much about who she is. The cup a character drinks from can be telling, as well, just as the magazine a character reads can. How Laura deals with her little lamb will reveal character. The size, shape, texture, and weight of the lamb can affect the kind of choices the actor will be able to make. None of this should be left to chance. You must always approach your work armed with the idea that everything counts. That includes what props to use and how to use them.

The areas of movement and voice for actors are vast and can be studied as their own disciplines. And they are studied, of course, in many college and graduate programs. But you can begin exploring your character's physicality and vocal characteristics right now. Here follows a brief list of items that you might want to start thinking about as you begin dealing with your character's traits:

Voice

Pitch

Tempo

Rhythm

Loudness

Fluidity versus haltingness

Movement

Energy center (head, hips, abdomen)

Size of movements

Speed of movement

Grace

Level of stillness versus activity

The character's basic walk

My Laura, for instance, will have:

a quiet, breathy voice, that is low pitched as if always trying to hide inside her. She will speak haltingly as though words do not come easily to her. Only on the rare occasions when she gets enthused will the pitch of her voice rise and the haltingness disappear. This will not happen in my scene, however. Laura's energy center will be low, and her posture will be bad, shoulders drooped and concave—as though all of her energy is driving her downward and inward, and as if all her available energy goes to keeping her bad leg in check. She will walk slowly and carefully, always trying to avoid a sudden slip that would draw unnecessary attention to her. Only when comfortably planted will her posture lengthen and become almost pretty. This will happen as she isolates herself within the world of her menagerie in my scene. Her movements will be small, because in stillness there is safety.

Notice that I have made specific choices for my character's physicality and vocal qualities. I have also provided a written justification for my choices. These choices are consistent with what we know about the character and will serve to amplify those characteristics in the scene.

Since this exercise covers so much ground, you probably won't successfully hit all the marks. However, you will probably learn much more from what you haven't yet mastered than from what you have. Regardless of how much time you actually have to spend on it, this exercise can go a long way in helping you independently discover and tell the story of the play and of your character. You can apply much of what you learn here the next time you do scene work in class, or, more importantly, the next time you work on a role in production. And that, of course, is the ultimate purpose for most of what you do whenever you're trying to learn the craft behind the art of acting.

READING THE MAP—SCRIPT TO GOLD

SO FAR, WE HAVE FOCUSED ON TELLING THE STORY BASED on an analysis of the script and converting that analysis into physical choices that make the story clear. At times the planning and suggested execution of action has been so specific that the work might seem more like choreography than acting—a seeming contradiction to an art form that supposedly mirrors the spontaneity of real life. Of course, the implication in the work described is that once the initial choices have been made, the rehearsal process, again like choreography, will permit the actor to become so comfortable. With time and repetition, these choices will no longer be thought about at all, and the actor will be able to can focus totally in the moment and develop the next layer of the work.

Unfortunately, this kind of process bucks many students' preset ideas about what acting is. For them, maybe like you, acting is about playing character, becoming one with the character, allowing the character to dictate the choices made as actors. They expect that once an actor has the tools the acting teacher will provide, an actor will become the character in much the same way a Ouija Board invites a spirit to take over the game. Spontaneously, they think, a character's spirit will appear, crawl inside the actor's body, and navigate the choices. So true is this spirit that its choices and needs transcend in importance that of the playwright's intentions, and, perhaps, even those of the director.

Expectations like these are reinforced regularly on my favorite interview show and the only one totally dedicated to the actor's craft — *Inside the Actors Studio*. Meryl Streep, a personal icon and a wonderful character actress, during her interview confessed that she can't discuss her technique because she doesn't really know what happens to her when she works, but it's something magical. And Billy Bob Thornton, one of today's most brilliant and chameleon-like character actors, says that he barely reads the script before the camera is turned on. He doesn't want the script to interfere with his creativity. At least megastar and underrated actor Tom Cruise admits to doing enormous amounts of research before he gets in front of the camera. Yet he, too, makes no specific choices about what he will do before the camera rolls. He trusts that his preparation will spontaneously take him where he needs to go.

Since I have great admiration for the work of all of these actors, I certainly cannot say that their technique is wrong. Whatever works, works. Of course, these interviews, for the most part, focus on film acting, and in film the director shapes the story through editing and the actor has many chances to give her what she needs. Onstage, every moment counts in performance and there are no second chances. Theater actors create and maintain the logical progression of story from moment to moment.

If you are an actor just beginning your own journey, and you haven't yet discovered that your intuitive genius is a totally reliable instrument, then approaching character from the outside in, and using analysis, planning, and choice making for your essential physical, emotional, and psychological makeup, may be the way to go. You may also want to start treating the idea of fully inhabiting a character as something that might or might not happen, rather than making it your ultimate goal. If you accept that doing so will not compromise the virtue of your work, you will be on your way to the creation of a useful, reliable approach.

As a basic premise, keep in mind that your responsibility as an actor, first and foremost, is to help tell the story of the play. The playwright has written your character as one of the cogs in the storytelling process. The play is not just about you, not just about your character — even when your character's name is the play's title. Your Hamlet, your Hedda, your Sweeney Todd must serve the story being told. Yes, of course your character has a story to tell, as well, but it will never be at the expense of the play or the production's overall story. You must do your job in terms of the bigger picture, first and always. Many actors, even on *Inside the Actors Studio,* have confirmed this philosophy. Harrison Ford, for instance, said his job was to "move the story along." What he does is to "take the script, study the story," and see what he can do to "make his character advance the story."

Your first responsibility, then, is to read and decipher the play as written. Acting, in spite of what you may want to believe, starts with reading. Being able to read and interpret what the playwright has written is of primary importance. Even in a film, an actor with an approach like Billy Bob Thornton's has to be able to read the scripts he is offered and decide whether there is anything in there worth doing. For most actors, however, the need goes much further. If you have gotten this far in your pursuit of a career as an actor and cannot read, or cannot read well, you are at a tremendous disadvantage — both in terms of delivering the words and in terms of analysis. You will have to master reading as part of the mastery of your craft. Here we will focus on the analysis skills that go along with reading well.

In the following paragraphs I've provided a list of questions that you should be able to answer after reading a script. The answers to these questions will provide you with a stepping-off point for the development of your character. You should watch for these things as you read. Keep in mind that it may take several readings before all the answers fall in place. On a first read, you might just want to go along for the ride, by simply reacting to the play and seeing how it strikes you, but eventually you will have to go further, much further. You must learn to read actively — questioning all through the process why things happen as they do, why things are said the way they are said, why the playwright sets up scenes the way she does.

Take nothing at face value. A good playwright does what she does for particular reasons. Try to figure out what those reasons are. You may not like or agree with everything you read. That may be because at this point you do not fully understand the playwright's total intention; you may change your mind as you get deeper into the process. Or it may be because your taste is not in line with this particular playwright's work. Either way, your obligation remains — to create your character and serve the play to the best of your capabilities.

Here are some preliminary questions you should address during your initial readings:

What kind of play is this (genre)? Drama, melodrama, comedy, tragedy, farce, etc.? How will its genre affect how the story will be told?

Do you understand the world of the play? What style of acting might be required to tell the story effectively? Realism, theatricalism, absurdism, etc.?

Do you understand the story being told? Do you understand its dramatic progression?

Do the characters make sense in their storytelling roles?

Do you understand the meaning of the play, the playwright's intent in writing it? What dialogue, action, character choices, stage direction, etc. help the play's meaning come across to you?

Do you understand the language of the play? Is it different than the way we speak in everyday life? Why? How? Does that change the way you will need to act your role?

Do you understand the world of the play? Is it a different world than the world we live in? How is it different? How does that difference serve the playwright's meaning? How might it affect your acting?

Do you understand the other elements the playwright has written into the play and how they contribute to the story and its meaning?

If you are ready to buy into the premise that your character serves the story, then your character analysis should begin with the story itself. To understand the story, you must understand its conflict, its dramatic progression, and the roles its various characters play. You must understand the language and how the various characters use it. You must understand the world the playwright has created in this particular play. You must figure out why the playwright is telling this particular story and what he wants the audience to walk away with after seeing the play.

Let's say by way of example that you're beginning to work on *The Three Sisters* by Anton Chekhov. He called his major plays "comedies," though you might think after reading his major works that they are more sad than funny. For more than a hundred years, directors and actors have been arguing over the best way to make Chekhov work effectively for audiences while serving the playwright's intention. There is no right or wrong here, there is only effective drama onstage. You must ultimately make your choices based on decisions agreed upon by the director and his production team regarding the world of the play and its genre. Whether or not you totally agree with those decisions, you must help create a unified world. If it works for an audience, then it works, but these are not your decisions to make.

What we can agree on here, however, is that any Chekhov play offers a limited amount of plot, and most of its conflict and its situation are character-driven. A character-driven play never contains a lot of action. Instead, the characters' unfolding dreams and desires — and the surprising things we learn about them as the onion skin covering their souls is removed — hold our attention. In addition, characters in a Chekhov play tend to not express their thoughts and emotions directly. The high personal stakes and interpersonal conflicts are masked through dialogue that may be superficial yet disguise a deep well of emotional conflict. You will have to look closely to see how each of the characters is related by blood and by emotion to the next. You must discover as much of this as possible in the play. If you begin your reading knowing nothing about a Chekhovian play, you might miss the boat altogether.

In addition, the world of Chekhov is an alien one compared to twenty-first-century American life, yet the play's world is true to the lives led and beliefs held by the gentry class of provincial Russia at the turn of the nineteenth century. It is your responsibility as an actor to understand the necessary historical and sociological background information. It informs the play, and it will inform your reading of it. By the same token, Chekhov comments on the society he writes about through the actions and comments of his characters. Knowing something about what he is trying to say can help you understand the plays' meaning and lead you to choices that will help you create character.

Whether you're working on a Chekhov play or something by a contemporary author, you must leave no stone unturned. You'll find gold under those rocks. Doing your research is an essential part of your journey. If you were to play a surgeon on a television show, or a beat cop, you would consider it your job to see what real doctors and policemen do in the situation you will be portraying. It is no different when you are handling the analysis part of your journey to performance. You must do the necessary work with your script. Even if you read the play several times, it is not likely that you will be able to answer all of the questions listed earlier in this chapter without doing this kind of background homework, and a lot of it. You will also need to do a good deal of critical thinking, using what you have learned from your research.

Besides knowing about the playwright and how she thinks and feels, you will need to use the information you find to understand how the story is intended to operate on the audience. Sometimes reading reviews of other productions of a play, in addition to reading critical writing about it, can help you here. But eventually, it will be necessary to examine the play from the point of view of the audience to determine how it will best work from their eyes. Remember that the audience is watching the whole play unfold, while you as an actor playing a character will ultimately be viewing the story from a particular vantage point. Keep in mind that the work is ultimately intended for the audience. Any choices you make must be made with that story and that audience in mind.

Only after you understand the play from both the playwright's point of view and the audience's are you ready to ask yourself specific questions about your character, starting with how your character serves the story. By going through this process, you will create, develop, and shape your individual performance such that it serves the playwright, the audience, and your individual artistry. Remember that character is created onstage primarily by what you do as an actor and the manner in which you do it. The exterior physicality of character is also important, of course. But the externals of character are in part taken care of by the costume designed for your character and how you use it.

The remaining aspects of the physical character need to be created and executed by you. These characteristics will include the way you move, walk, talk, gesture, and focus your attention. Your tempo, rhythm, pace, and energy level will be equally important. Many other physical characteristics may be necessary, or you may be so well cast in a role that you can operate primarily from your basic self. It depends on the play and on the role. But all externals you develop for your character are secondary when compared to the importance of the actions you choose and the manner in which you carry them out.

Before we leave this overview, however, let's take a look at the outline that follows. It serves as a map of the kinds of things you might want to consider as part of your overall analysis of any play you'll be working on as an actor. You will find it far more specific than the general discussion questions listed earlier. Remember, the issues addressed by the outline should be considered only after you have done your preliminary reading and analysis regarding the story and how it works. You will find some of the items here more important than others, depending on the script you are working from. But each of these items can help steer your thinking toward finding insights that will effectively serve your ultimate performance. I have divided the outline according to Aristotle's six basic elements of drama. All of these elements will be found in any play to varying degrees and levels of importance depending on the particular work.

Before beginning any detailed analysis, however, keep in mind that you must understand the kind of play you are in (its genre) and the specific world the play exists in. This world may require a unified specific style from the play's actors in order to create this world.

A play belongs to a particular genre when it shares a set of particular characteristics. Some basic types include

Tragedy

Comedy

Drama

Farce

Melodrama

Each of these genres has its own set of characteristics. A play may follow these characteristics specifically, or it may be a hybrid of one or more types. It is helpful to understand the kind of play you will be involved in. You will need to fulfill certain obligations when you make choices about your work that are consistent with the play's structure and purpose.

The playwright will also have created a particular world for the play that may require a specific acting style to bring it to life. These worlds can be described as "-isms,"including:

Realism

Theatricalism

Expressionism

Absurdism

Ultimately it will be your responsibility to make choices that are consistent with those of the other actors and with the world being created by the director and her production team if the play is to work as a whole. The following outline can help you think in terms of the world of the play. It will help you define the world your character will exist in.

Consider the following:

I. Action or Plot
    A. Given circumstances—the who, the what, the when, the where
        1. Time—century, decade, year, season, month, day, time of day
        2. Place—geographical locale, specific locale, specifics of the production set
        3. Social structure of the play's world—includes the culture and customs, family hierarchy and traditions, social classes, occupations, etiquette, relationship of characters, and accepted manners
        4. Economic system of the time in that particular society
        5. Politics and law
        6. Science and culture
        7. Religious beliefs
        8. The world of the play
    B. Backstory—what must be understood if the play is to work
        1. How the story unfolds
            a. a plot that is hidden and is revealed only as needed (modern)
            b. a plot in which the background information is clearly laid out at the beginning before the plot thickens
            c. the arc of the story
        2. Dramatic road markers
            a. important plot points—the stepping stones in the arc of the story
            b. important character moments—the stepping stones in the arc of character revelation
    C. Plot: physical and psychological action

1. Physical action — the physical things that happen onstage
    a. entrances and exits
    b. blocking
    c. use of props
    d. specific physical activities
2. Psychological action — conflicts, needs, wins, losses, discoveries made by characters that move the plot forward

D. Plot: mechanics of action set up by the playwright
    1. Progression
        a. moments
        b. beats
        c. scenes
        d. acts
    2. Structure
        a. conflicts
        b. plot or plotlines and how they parallel and/or connect
        c. point of attack (place where story begins in relation to backstory)
        d. inciting action — the specific incident (if there is one) that actually causes the plot to kick in
        e. moments of complication and obstacles
        f. climax
        g. resolution

II. Character
    A. Conflicts
    B. Dramatic action — arc of individual character action — moments of wins losses, discoveries, etc.
    C. Objectives, needs, wants, goals, etc.
    D. Willpower — what character is willing to do to get what he needs
    E. Values — things most important, least important, ethics, values, etc.
    F. Personality traits
    G. Physical characteristics

H. Complexity (how much characters perceive about themselves and their situations)

I. Relationships with other characters

III. Idea or spine — the play's meaning and how it is brought out in the play

A. What is the play's main idea?

B. Characters' contribution to idea

C. Plot's contribution to idea

D. Dialogue's contribution to idea

IV. Dialogue

A. Words characters use

B. Sentence structure used by characters

C. Speech constructions

D. Special qualities

E. Theatricality of language

V. Music: tempo, rhythm, mood — in the dialogue and construction of the action

A. Sensing its use and presence

B. Places it changes and why

C. Using it effectively

VI. Spectacle — h.ow they relate to the story and to the characters

A. Sets

B. Props

C. Costumes

D. Lights

In the chapter that follows, we will take a closer look at the work you'll need to do to create a believable and compelling character through action that serves the playwright's story, the audience, and your own artistic aspirations.

CHAPTER

SEVEN

FOLLOWING THE MAP—ANALYSIS TO ACTION

WHEN I WAS A KID, FANTASIZING ABOUT WHAT IT MIGHT be like to be an actor, I always had this image of myself being handed a script by some big director, taking a few moments to look the dialogue over, and then confidently striding over to where the camera was set up. Moments later, I'd be offered a contract by the director based simply on what he had just seen from the other side of the lens. My brilliance and charisma could not be denied. All it took was a quick familiarization with the material and my talent did the rest.

Maybe you have had similar fantasies, or maybe that is precisely the way you operate as an actor. Your instincts are so sharp, so accurate, that you need not spend much time with the script before you're ready to use it, or even transcend it, as the case may be. The script, for you, is merely the stepping stone that allows you to inspire yourself and propel your art out there for the waiting masses. If this is you, my sincerest congratulations. Unfortunately, for most of us, this is not the typical scenario.

I sometimes wonder what Elia Kazan saw at Marlon Brando's audition for *A Streetcar Named Desire,* and how different the audition was compared to what Stanley looked and sounded like by opening night on Broadway. And even if Brando conjured up hints on audition day of what the final product was to become, I wonder whether it resulted from luck or serendipitous casting, or whether Brando had actually made some good, well-thought-out choices before the audition—choices that contributed to the clarity of the character and action of the play. Choices that netted, for him, the role of a lifetime. Even if Brando did come up with some amazing Stanley choices when he first read for the role, he must have made literally thousands of choices between that audition and the first performance for an audience weeks later, choices that would eventually immortalize him. And he, of course, had Elia Kazan, one of America's greatest theater and film directors, to guide him, challenge him, and flatter him into that legendary performance.

Most of us will not be working with a Kazan or a Brando anytime soon. And there is never a guarantee that we will end up working with people who elevate our own game simply by virtue of how good *they* are. So, if you are not necessarily going to succeed through your natural, spontaneous brilliance, or the brilliance of those who surround you, then what exactly will you have to do to produce the necessary goods? The answer starts with what so many fine actors have learned to do—analyze a script effectively. Only then will you be certain that the choices you make are clear, exciting, and serve the story you are telling.

So the question is—do you have the skills to examine a script in a way that will give you a road map for what to do, keeping in mind that your primary job is to serve the script by telling its story effectively? When you talk about the character you will play, by the way, do you think of that character in terms of how she serves the script she is in, or do you think of her as a separate entity who happens to function within the play? If it is the latter, you will need to adjust your thinking. Your character was written by the playwright to help tell his story. Every character in a play makes a contribution to that telling. That is a character's primary function. Many actors, especially untrained ones, mistakenly believe that a play's story is there to provide a framework for their characters. This kind of thinking can ruin a play.

The story holds the play together. The story consists of its characters, its action, its dialogue, and the manner in which that story is told, including its tone and narrative viewpoint. No individual ingredient can ever be more important than the combination of parts. No one ever eats a cake for the eggs that are in it, any more than an audience would come to see a play just to watch an individual character. Characters in the context of a play's action are why an audience is willing to sit and watch. And few characters and fewer performances are so compelling, so absorbing, or so amusing that an audience will commit to watching them for two hours unless the question "What is going to happen next?" somehow figures into the quotient. Playwrights want their work to be successful. They know story is essential. Therefore, if you read a play and can't find the story to hang your choices on, there is either a problem with the play or with your reading of it. If the play you're working on is an established one, then the problem likely lies with you.

The reality of today's professional theatre is this: money is tight, so rehearsal periods are too short. Actors therefore must be able to prepare on their own. They must come to rehearsals with the goods in hand, not as blank slates. The rehearsal time frame probably won't provide the actor time for improvisation, trial and error, and extended exploration. You will have to learn and master now how to do these things on your own. It will take time and effort. It will take discipline. You will need to learn how to read as an actor must — carefully and actively. You will need to learn to ask the questions necessary of the script and of the playwright who wrote that script. If you begin with the premise that everything the playwright wrote into her script is there for a reason, you will have the motivation to take everything you see on the printed page as a clue to doing your job as an actor effectively.

Some of the things you will have to think about, certainly at the beginning stages of your analysis, include everything that appeared in the outline in the last chapter. Here is a more condensed set of issues you can sink your teeth into:

- given circumstances — the who, what, when, and where of the play. The more specifically you define them, the more specific your choices will become. Choices that are specific are more likely to be clear and compelling. Generalized choices will not be.
- story — the narrative produced when character, plot, and dialogue are combined, producing a particular effect, feeling, or idea, or all three.
- arc or throughline — the map of the journey a character makes through a story. It can be literal or figurative, in that it marks the changes a character undergoes during the course of the action and provides moments that are dramatic and revealing.
- conflict — the engine of drama, created when the opposing forces that make a story interesting square off.

- objective — what the character needs and pursues at all times, resulting from the conflict the playwright creates.
- moments — specific islands of import in the story's progression or arc; places in the script where moments can be made, revealed, and/or portrayed dramatically. Victories, defeats, and discoveries are often made there.
- physical actions — the things the actor chooses to do physically to make thought and feelings clear.

We'll take a look at all these items more closely a bit later, but for now let's just work on an overview.

Below you will find the one-act play *Eye to Eye*, by Chris Graybill. This spare three-character play consists primarily of dialogue between a man and a woman in a restaurant. The third character — a waiter — is not central to the action, though he manages to comment on it. Despite the play's brevity, we come to know both main characters well enough to have an emotional response to them and to the situation they find themselves in by the time the play is over. How the playwright accomplishes all this in so small a box is actually quite impressive. Needless to say, before an actor can make any decisions about character and action, it will be necessary to read and understand the entire play and how the elements all work together.

Read the play and see what you can learn about its given circumstances (the who, what, when, and where of the script) and its action. Just use what you find in the script and see what you can come up with. As you read, you might want to underline, highlight, or jot down phrases that give you clues.

Once you have accumulated your list, go back over it, and think about the significance of each clue you have chosen to list. We'll compare notes after you have completed your investigation. Read the play as many times as you want or need to. Remember, multiple, careful readings are essential for an actor to accumulate necessary information. Consider yourself a detective on the case. If you read multiple times — and a serious actor would — try reading from several points of view, — from the author's, from the audience's, from each of the character's. See what you learn from each and put your thoughts together.

EYE TO EYE

CHARACTERS
Man
Woman
Waiter

TIME AND PLACE
A restaurant. The present.

[As the play opens, the Man and Woman have finished dinner at a
fashionable restaurant. He reaches across the table toward her hand,
though He does not touch her, and gazes into her eyes.]

Woman: That's enough.
Man: What's enough?
Woman: Stop, please.
Man: Stop what?
Woman: Looking at me.
Man: I like looking at you.
Woman: I can see that.
Man: Don't you like it?
Woman: Sort of.
Man: You like it. You love it.
Woman: Up to a point.
Man: Set by you?
Woman: Who else?

[Beat.]

Man: So you don't like my looks. I like yours. There are flecks of
brown in your right eye. Did you know that?
Woman: Yes.
Man: They are beautiful, your eyes.

WOMAN: Only the part you can see. My eyeballs are red-veined, elongated bulbs of jelly. Just like yours.

MAN: Please, I just ate. How come it bothers you? My looking at you. No, really. I'm interested.

WOMAN: It's too intimate.

MAN: Intimate? We're just sitting here. Having coffee. I'm way over here.

WOMAN: There's something in your eye.

MAN: What?

WOMAN: I can't quite recognize it.

MAN: Something in my eye. Let me see now. Is it a gnat?

WOMAN: No.

MAN: An eyelash?

WOMAN: It's something hidden.

MAN: Something warm? Something cool? Something sexy?

WOMAN: Not exactly.

MAN: Bedroom eyes?

WOMAN: More than that.

MAN: That's interesting. That's very, very interesting.

[WAITER *enters.*]

WAITER: How was everything this evening?

WOMAN: Fine, thank you.

MAN: Fascinating.

WAITER: Can I bring you anything else?

MAN: I'd like more coffee.

WOMAN: Just the check, please.

[WAITER *nods and exits.*]

MAN: You double-parked?

WOMAN: Hmmm.

[*They sit briefly in silence until the* WAITER *returns.*]

WAITER: Here we are. [HE *refills* MAN'*s cup and leaves check.*] I'll take that whenever you're ready. [HE *exits.*]

WOMAN: [*Picking up check.*] I'll get this.

MAN: No, my treat. [HE *snatches the check from her hand.*]

WOMAN: Why don't we split it?

MAN: No, no, no, no. I treat you, then you treat me. That's the way it works around here.

WOMAN: I really would rather …

MAN: You're welcome. [HE *takes a credit card out of his wallet and places it on top of the bill.*] You can get it next time.

WOMAN: Wait a minute. You better let me split it now. There isn't going to be a next time.

[*They look at each other a moment.*]

MAN: I see. OK. Tell you what. I've got a deal for you.

WOMAN: No, thanks.

MAN: A sporting proposition.

WOMAN: How much is my half?

[*During the following exchange,* SHE *repeatedly reaches for the check, and* HE *holds it away.*]

MAN: No, no. Let's do this fair and square. We both want to pay. We'll compete for it. Loser pays.

WOMAN: This is a boy's game.

MAN: We'll have a looking contest. Whoever breaks eye contact first, loses. [*Pause.*] Well?

WOMAN: Loser pays the check?

MAN: Bingo.

WOMAN: You're on. Ready?

MAN: Wait a minute. Let me get loose here. [*Does facial and neck exercises.*] The World Eyeballing Championships. All right. The Kid is ready. Here we go. On your mark, get set, stare!

WOMAN: [*Immediately averting her eyes.*] OK, I lose, Give me the check.

MAN: Oh, no. Time out.

WOMAN: I lost, fair and square. Hand it over.

MAN: No. I see what's happening here. I get it. We're going to have to revise the rules. *Winner* picks up the check.

WOMAN: I really want to leave.

MAN: Then leave! Walk out! Allow me the great honor of paying for you. Let me treat you. It would be my pleasure. [*Pause.*] Are you going to play or not?

WOMAN: I'll play.

[SHE *takes out her credit card.* THEY *lay their gold American Express cards on the table.*]

MAN: Ah, victory. Gold vs. gold. At last we see eye to eye.

WOMAN: Just start.

MAN: Go!

[THEY *begin.*]

MAN: Ho, ho, what a glare. Daggers, bullets. You won't be able to keep that up for long. You know what you look like?

WOMAN: Do you have to talk?

MAN: Why not? Nobody said anything about talking. There's nothing in the rules about talking. As I was saying, you look like one of those gargoyles whose stare turns men to stone.

WOMAN: Gorgon.

MAN: What?

WOMAN: It's a Gorgon, not a gargoyle.

MAN: Well, you must be a Gorgon because you are definitely turning me to stone.

WOMAN: You feel something getting hard?

MAN: Absolutely.

WOMAN: Maybe it's your arteries.

MAN: Ho, ho. Very good. But you don't get any style points.

[WAITER *enters, notices their intensity and hesitates.*]

WAITER: Can I take that for you? [*No response.*] No problem. Just let me know when you're ready. [HE *exits.*]

MAN: Your eyes are quivering. You're blinking fast. It won't be long now. Any second now you'll lose it. Ha, you looked away.

WOMAN: I did not.

MAN: Almost. You will.

WOMAN: Everything is a covert operation with men, isn't it?

MAN: Don't lecture me about "men."

WOMAN: All right, you. Let's talk about you. Nothing can be straightforward with you. It's all innuendo.

MAN: I never said that.

WOMAN: Your secret weapon is secrecy. You think what's unspoken is the biggest threat there is. But you're wrong.

MAN: Cheap shots. Nothing but cheap shots.

WOMAN: You never say what's on your mind.

MAN: How would you know?

WOMAN: I can see it in your eyes. Oh, it's not sex. I see that now. Sex is for teenagers. You're way past that.

MAN: What is it then?

WOMAN: I don't think you want me to say it.

MAN: Go ahead.

WOMAN: Not out loud

MAN: As loud as you want.

WOMAN: Control. Domination. That's what's been in your eyes.

MAN: Is that the best you can do?

WOMAN: Sex is your means, not your end. [*Louder.*] You're thinking. I want to fuck this woman.

MAN: No fair.

WOMAN: [*Louder.*] I want to fuck her into submission.

WAITER: [*Enters anxiously.*] Are we OK here? Can I take that for you? Sir?

[MAN *looks up at* WAITER.]

WOMAN: You lose.

[MAN *hesitates, holding the check. Then* HE *reaches to take her credit card, and* SHE *hands it to him.*]

81

MAN: Add fifteen percent.
WOMAN: I'll tell him how much to add. Add twenty percent.

[MAN *gives him the check and a credit card, and* WAITER *exits.*]

MAN: Don't gloat.
WOMAN: Why not? I won.
MAN: You had to cheat.
WOMAN: There are no rules.
MAN: You don't really believe that.
WOMAN: I told the truth. That's the ultimate weapon.
MAN: If you call truth a weapon, you are pretty far gone.

[WAITER *returns with a salver holding credit card and invoice.* HE *lays it beside the* MAN *and exits.*]

WOMAN: You all stick together, don't you?

[SHE *takes the invoice.* HE *picks up the credit card off the tray and plays with it, as* SHE *bends to sign.*]

MAN: Look me in the eye and tell me you're proud of what you did.
WOMAN: I am very, very proud. I thought this would be another night to forget. With another bitter, predictable prick. But I was wrong. I want to remember this. When my statement comes, I'm going to frame it and put it on my wall. Every time I look at it, I'll think of you. [SHE *signs the slip and tears off her copy.*] Could I have my card?

[HE *hands it to her.*]

WOMAN: So long, loser. [SHE *exits.*]

[MAN *stares thoughtfully at his coffee.* WAITER *enters and picks up the credit card invoice.*]

WAITER: Sir, there's some mix-up here. This isn't your signature.

MAN: I know.

WAITER: Your friend *signed* on your credit card?

MAN: She must have thought I gave you hers. She'll see her mistake when she gets her statement.

WAITER: Shall I run your card through again?

MAN: "There are no rules." Everybody says that. But they don't accept it. Not down deep. [HE *tears up the credit slip and hands his card to* WAITER.] And do it right this time.

WAITER: Sir?

MAN: You added twenty-five percent. After she said twenty. Make it fifteen. Exactly. Because I've got my eye on you.

[*Curtain.*]

THE END

If you didn't compile your own clue list, examine the one that follows and see if you can determine why I included the items I did. If you have compiled a list, compare yours to the one that follows and see if you can figure out why there are differences. There are no rights or wrongs here, only pieces of information that will help us understand the characters and the story and, later, to make choices—choices that will help tell the story effectively.

Here is my list:

The present.

A fashionable restaurant.

The MAN *and* WOMAN *have finished dinner.*

HE *reaches across the table toward her hand though* HE *does not touch her and gazes into her eyes.*

That's enough.

Stop, please.

Looking at me.

I like looking at you.

You like it. You love it.

Up to a point.

So you don't like my looks. I like yours.

It's too intimate.

There's something in your eye.

It's something hidden.

Bedroom eyes.

I'll get this.

No, my treat.

Why don't we split it.

I treat you, then you treat me. That's the way it works around here.

You're welcome.

HE *takes a credit card out of his wallet and places it on top of the bill.*

You better let me split it now. There isn't going to be a next time.

I see.

I've got a deal for you.

A sporting proposition.

During the following exchange, SHE *repeatedly reaches for the check, and* HE *holds it away.*

We'll compete. Loser pays.

This is a boy's game.

Whoever breaks eye contact first, loses.

Immediately averting her eyes.

Okay, I lose. Give me the check.

We're going to have to revise the rules. *Winner* picks up the check.

SHE *takes out her credit card.* THEY *lay their gold American Express cards on the table.*

Gold versus gold. At last we see eye to eye.

Daggers, bullets.

Do you have to talk?

There's nothing in the rules about talking.

As I was saying, you look like one of those gargoyles whose stare turns men to stone.

Gorgon.

You feel something getting hard?

Absolutely.

WAITER *enters, notices their intensity and hesitates.*

You looked away./I did not./Almost. You will.

Everything is a covert operation with men, isn't it?

Nothing can be straightforward with you. It's all innuendo.

Your secret weapon is secrecy. You think what's unspoken is the biggest threat there is.

Control. Domination. That's what's been in your eyes.

Sex is your means, not your end.

Louder.

You're thinking. I want to fuck this woman.

I want to fuck her into submission.

You lose.

MAN *hesitates, holding the check. Then* HE *reaches to take her credit card, and* SHE *hands it to him.*

Add fifteen percent.

I'll tell him how much to add. Add twenty percent.

Don't gloat.

Why not? I won.

You had to cheat.

There are no rules.

I told the truth. That's the ultimate weapon.

WAITER *returns with a salver holding credit card and invoice.* HE *lays it beside the* MAN *and exits.*

You all stick together, don't you?

SHE *takes the invoice.* HE *picks up the credit card off the tray and plays with it, as* SHE *bends to sign.*

Look me in the eye and tell me you're proud of what you did.

I am very, very proud.

With another bitter, predictable prick.

When my statement comes, I'm going to frame it and put it on my wall.

So long, loser.

Your friend signed on *your* credit card?

She'll see her mistake when she gets her statement.

"There are no rules." Everybody says that. But they don't accept it.

HE *tears up the credit slip and hands his card to* WAITER.

Do it right this time.

You added twenty-five percent. After she said twenty. Make it fifteen. Exactly. Because I've got my eye on you.

What do the items on the list tell us about the man and the woman? About their relationship? About their short history together? About their individual lives? About their feelings toward each other? About each other's genders? About their values? What do they tell us about the current situation? About their needs? What changes occur during the course of the play regarding these issues and any other important issues that apply? Do the characters seem different at the end of the play than they did at the beginning? How so? How and why did these changes occur? Did the characters really change, or was the change your perception of them? What is the difference, and why might that distinction be important to telling the story well? Look at these changes closely and try to determine what they tell us about the story, and about the characters, about the meaning of the play. What is the tone of the piece? Is it funny? Dramatic? A combination? And so on.

Notice that my clues came from both the dialogue and from the stage directions. It is fair and wise to use everything available for your analysis. My list could have been much longer. In fact, I might have included everything in the script. We know by now that everything in a good script is there for a reason. Further, actions, implied or actual, in a script can be every bit as useful for analysis as dialogue. We can sometimes learn about a play's story and its characters through what the author tells us directly through commentary and stage direction. This is certainly true with *Eye to Eye,* where the playwright tells us quite a bit directly in his terse but telling stage directions. More often, however, we learn through what the characters say, what other characters say about them, and through what they do, implied but not necessarily stated by the playwright. Sometimes we must look beyond the literal meaning of what is said, as well, and figure out what the clues tell us through their implication. Note, for instance, the implication in the repeated references to looks and looking at each other. You might ask yourself what these repeated references do to and for the man and the woman or, for that matter, the waiter, who is often described as looking on. The answer will give you clues as to the story's progression and meaning.

It might be a worthwhile exercise to note, from my list or from your own, which clues refer to the man, to the woman, and to the progressive action of the story. You might want to rearrange your list into those categories. Once you do, you may discover that seeing these clues listed together will begin to provide a nice composite of character and a suggested map of the sequential movement in the story. Keep in mind that, ultimately, all things said and done must be examined carefully.

All right, now that you have collected your information and determined the significance of the individual items you accumulated, study your clue sheet and mine and try to figure out what it all adds up to. String together all the evidence and actually make a composite of the story and characters. Doing this will give you a map to use later, when you will need to begin a more detailed examination of the action of the play. See if you can put what you have learned into a few paragraphs that, when read, will get to the essence of who the man and the woman are, and, if possible, who the waiter is. Most importantly, be sure to describe the action contained in the play as you understand it. Only through character and especially through a play's action will we get to its meaning. But keep in mind that a play's meaning will surface through the story. Note that even character names can give clues. Why, for instance, did Chris Graybill not give his characters actual names in this play?

When you have finished, compare your composite to the one that follows:

A man and a woman, both attractive and successful, are concluding their dinner—a first date at an upscale restaurant. The man tries to come on to the woman by staring at her, reaching for her, and by praising her attractiveness. She rejects him gently at first but then tells him that he is too forward and implies he should back off. He presses her, and she tells him there is something in his eyes that puts her off. The waiter interrupts, offering coffee, but the woman asks for the check instead and wants to pay. The man insists that he will pay the check and physically takes control of the bill. He tells her that she can pay the next time. She tells him there will be no next time.

The woman tries several times unsuccessfully to take the bill from the man. They look at each other, and he then offers a staring contest to determine who will pay the bill. After failing again to take possession of the check, the woman agrees and then proceeds to lose on purpose. The man claims foul and insists they do it again with the winner paying. The woman threatens to leave. The man calls her bluff by saying that if she leaves, he gets to pay the check. The woman agrees to the contest. They both lay their gold American Express cards on the table. They play. The man talks trash during the contest, trying to distract the woman into averting her eyes. He even goes for the dirty joke. The waiter interrupts again but quickly removes himself when he sees the intensity of the situation. The man continues to talk trash, and the woman accuses him of acting in a covert, indirect way like all men do. The man calls her on her stereotyping of men, so she makes the accusation specific to him. She then accuses him of wanting sex only as a control thing. The man pushes her further. She is about to lose it when the waiter interrupts again, this time distracting the man, who averts his eyes. The woman calls his loss, and the man takes her credit card from her. He tells the waiter what to add as a tip, and she takes back control by adding more. The man passes a credit card to the waiter. The man accuses her of cheating. She counters with the fact that she is the one who tells the truth. The waiter returns and puts the check by the man. The woman notes that men always stick together. The man asks her to look him in the eyes and say that she is proud of her actions. She explodes with righteousness and venom toward him and men in general. She asks for her credit card. When he hands it back, she calls him a loser and exits.

The waiter returns and informs the man that the woman signed his card. The man gives the waiter his card again and tells the waiter to rip up the previous receipt. He also notes that the waiter had upped the tip to more than the woman asked for. In a final act of control, the man tells the waiter to reduce the tip to his original amount and warns the waiter that he has his eye on him.

How does your composite compare to this one? If yours is far different from mine, reexamine my clue list and your own, and see if you missed anything important that would bring you closer to the synopsis I have composed. Remember, the point is to use specifics from the script to draw conclusions about the story and characters. Everything stated in the description just provided is drawn from those specifics, either through the words or through actions. Sometimes the conclusions I have drawn are through implication rather than stated facts. Dialogue, as well as actions and stage direction, can imply information rather than spell it out. It is up to the actor to find important clues that may be covered up slightly or even deeply buried between the lines. The trick is to examine everything that is said and done, and figure out what it all adds up to. Keep in the forefront of your thinking that every word and action a playwright provides means something. Otherwise it wouldn't be there. Your job is to do the necessary detective work, because eventually it will be your responsibility to tell the story onstage, moment by moment, with all the clarity and punch you can give it.

It is always essential to keep in mind that a story consists of characters doing actions in sequential fashion. A story has a beginning, middle, and end with a central conflict or conflicts that will ensure an interesting journey from beginning to end. The characters who go on this story journey will be different at the end than they were at the beginning, because the journey somehow changes them. This change is apparent in *Eye to Eye*. As new information is revealed, our perceptions change, even as the characters' perceptions of each other evolve. The sequence of actions that the character undertakes and/or undergoes is called the character's *arc* or *throughline*.

A story also produces a desired effect on its audience if told correctly. It will be helpful if you know what that effect might be. What do you think the audience should be feeling by the end of *Eye to Eye*? Should the audience's feelings change during the journey? What are they at the beginning? Where, why, and how do they change? How do you know this?

The story will most likely also have a point that becomes clear as a result of the good telling. This point is often referred to as its *spine,* and all the elements of the story should work to support its spine. Does there seem to be a point to the story that unfolds in this play? What do you think the audience should be thinking about at the end of it? Does the play seem to present an issue for consideration? Does the playwright seem to have an attitude about that issue? Why do you think so? Knowing what this issue is and what the author is saying about it will help you make choices later on when you are called upon to do so.

A story also has a tone or mood that will help make it work effectively. What is the tone of *Eye to Eye*? Serious, comedic? A combination? Is it a comedy? Certainly it has its funny moments, but it also has some very serious overtones, doesn't it? What the play says—and how it says it—will affect how you ultimately play it. So, how do you think it should be played to work most effectively? These considerations must be addressed before you make and execute your final choices. As in the structure of most plays, the plot ends with an extremely dramatic action that leaves the audience with major feelings. Was the ending surprising to you? Should it be? Why? There is also some humor in the play. It will be important for you to know when and where it is supposed to be funny in order for you to help produce the desired effects yet not compromise the overall effect of the play.

With all this in mind, could you take me on the journey of the story found in *Eye to Eye*? By focusing on the action of the story, could you relate it in a step-by-step, chronological way? It is very important that you be able to do this.

In this play only two actors are onstage most of the time, so the storytelling gears will be equally shared by each of them. If those actors are going to tell the story effectively, they will need to know the moment-by-moment events — the momentary stories that occur when action combine with reaction. A good, clear story is produced when these moments occur in cause-and-effect fashion, one leading to the next. As an actor you must always play actions — if you are going to reveal the story clearly and sequentially. If you concern yourself only with the emotions involved, you are far less likely to be able to do this primary task.

There is also a third character in this play. His presence affects the behavior of the other two to some degree. Unlike the man and the woman, his wants and needs have little to do with what is going on between them. How *are* his needs affected by what occurs between them? How do his needs affect their needs? How do his needs affect the story? All these issues will have to be considered. Is the waiter visible throughout the play? Is this a choice to be made, or is it clear in the writing? If the waiter is present throughout the play, what effect would that have on the story and the telling of it? Would it be better for him to be present, or not? Why? Again, considerations to be addressed.

Keep in mind that actions are controllable and repeatable. They are also clear. Any emotional expression, no matter how deeply felt, is communicated to others more by its accompanying actions than any direct communication of the emotion itself. You are angry. You put your fist through a wall. The action and the manner in which you do it communicate your anger – the emotion is not put across directly. As an actor, if you rely on emotion to tell your story, you may be heartfelt and believable, compellingly so, but there is no guarantee that your work will be clear to an audience. For that reason, our focus should always be on actions. Emotions invariably follow a well-executed action, by the way. Put your fist through a wall with intensity, commit to the action, and a feeling indistinguishable from anger is likely to accompany it.

So find the actions and play them. The action in a story is like a set of dominoes stacked in a row and ready to be knocked over; once begun, one action leads to another in a cause-and-effect dynamic from the beginning of a script to its end. This juggernaut of action is a train any actor can ride to success. However, each of the cause-and-effect actions provided by the playwright will need to be clearly defined beforehand—if they are to be clearly executed once you put the play on its feet. If you can define these moments of action during your analysis, you will later be able to shape them clearly and fully when you need to enact them.

Take a few moments now and see if you can map out the action of the play, event by event. Finding the step-by-step action is harder than you might think. *Eye to Eye* contains both psychological and physical action—what the characters do through what they say and how they say it, and the things the characters actually do physically, respectively. The characters give and take, moment by moment. Some of the action is direct and clear, but some of it must be interpreted through implication. You will need to examine what the supplied physical action means in terms of the developing story, and you will need to consider all the dialogue very closely. Though some of the dialogue is literal, at times it must be dissected in terms of context and in terms of what the character really means *subtextually,* or under the surface of what is said.

Let's start with the play's simple sequence of action. Read through the play again, and as you do, jot down a chronological list of all the things that happen, noting how each event triggers the next. You might find it easier to see these cause-and-effect relationships if you start at the end of the play and work backward to the beginning. It is always easier to retrace your steps from the end of a maze than it is to get there. You are likely to find this to be the case with charting the action of a play, as well.

Once you have finished your chart, or *score* of the action, you will better understand the progression of the play and how all the pieces work together. You will have a map that reveals the sequence of events that make up the action of the story. Your score might look something like this:

MAN extends his hand across table toward WOMAN's hand.

MAN gazes into her eyes.

WOMAN asks him to stop looking at her.

Man questions her on why she does not want him to look at her.

Woman admits liking it somewhat.

Man compliments Woman on her eyes.

Woman confesses that Man's gazing is too intimate.

Woman admits that she doesn't like something in Man's eyes.

Man suggests it is his sexuality that makes her uncomfortable.

Waiter interrupts.

Man hints through Waiter that he finds Woman fascinating.

Woman asks for check.

Man challenges her rush to leave.

Waiter brings check.

Woman picks up check.

Man insists on paying.

Man snatches check from Woman.

They argue over check.

Man takes out credit card and puts it on bill.

Woman insists on splitting bill.

Woman declares there will be no next time.

They stare at each other.

Man offers deal.

Woman grabs for bill several times.

Man convinces her to play a staring contest for the bill.

Woman averts her eyes.

Man demands a replay in which winner gets to pay.

WOMAN threatens to leave.

MAN calls her bluff.

WOMAN agrees to play again.

MAN and WOMAN place credit cards on table.

MAN and WOMAN stare at each other.

MAN makes distracting talk.

MAN teases sexually.

WOMAN insults MAN's intelligence.

WAITER interrupts.

WAITER leaves.

WOMAN accuses men of acting deceitfully.

MAN accuses WOMAN of stereotyping.

WOMAN accuses MAN of being deceitful.

MAN defends himself and men.

WOMAN accuses MAN of using sex as tool to control and dominate.

WOMAN attacks MAN loudly.

WAITER interrupts.

MAN looks at WAITER.

WOMAN declares herself the winner.

MAN and WOMAN stare at each other.

WOMAN hands MAN her credit card.

MAN orders WAITER to take a 15 percent tip.

WOMAN orders WAITER to take a 20 percent tip.

MAN gives WAITER check and credit card.

WOMAN gloats.

MAN tells her not to.

WAITER brings check and puts it beside MAN.

WOMAN accuses men of sticking together.

MAN accuses WOMAN of being ashamed of her behavior.

WOMAN attacks MAN and his whole gender and says that she considers this a great victory.

WOMAN signs bill and leaves.

MAN stares.

WAITER returns. He examines signed bill. Informs MAN that WOMAN signed his credit card bill.

MAN tears up first credit card slip.

MAN orders WAITER to run bill through again correctly.

MAN warns WAITER to give himself the right tip amount this time — the original 15 percent.

MAN warns WAITER that he has his eyes on WAITER.

If you were to read this list back to yourself right now, you'd probably see the story unfold before your eyes. In essence, it is an effective map for the play. The action you've scored might have seemed apparent when you read it before, but without having this step-by-step guide in front of you, the story would probably be far less clear. You might even have ended up doing just what that bad joke teller does — forget important details or get the sequence balled up. Remember, your job is to get the playwright's story across. With a play-by-play map this specific, you're unlikely to get lost on your way to accomplishing your mission as an actor.

In the next chapter, we'll take an even closer look at the play, focusing on conflict — the engine of drama — and how it helps the actor determine his course of action. We'll also examine the step-by step action of this play more closely and then take a look at how finding the conflict in a play can help you make choices that will serve the script as well as the character you portray.

OBJECTIVE PLAYING—TOOL NUMBER ONE

AS ACTORS, WE MUST UNDERSTAND THE STORY OF THE PLAY, because ultimately, it is our job to make choices that will tell that story well. In fact, telling the story of the play is an actor's primary job. A playwright knows that for a story to work effectively, it must be planned out meticulously. If the playwright knows her craft, that is exactly what she will do. A good story is like a fine watch in which all the gears work together to keep the time precisely.

If you've ever tried to tell someone the story of the great movie you just saw, you know this is not always so easy. Though it was all clear to you when you saw it, getting those details right during your retelling can be a daunting task. If you have ever suffered through a story told by an excited friend who has no talent for storytelling, you know just what I mean. Forgotten or misplaced details fly at you like random machine-gun fire. You know those elements are important, but where they're coming from and why remain a mystery. The story's disorganized presentation keeps it from being clear or compelling. Or to put it another way, have you ever heard two people tell the same joke, one successfully, the next miserably? What is the difference? The good joke teller and the good storyteller keep the story ticking clearly and chronologically. The good storyteller also knows how to build the tension and keep you asking, "What will happen next?" To do your job effectively as an actor, you must know the storytelling gears and understand how they work together effectively.

In the previous chapter, we began our examination of a play for the following criteria:

- Given circumstances—the who, what, when, and where of the play. Specifically defined circumstances will likely be clear and compelling. Generalized choices will not.
- Story—the narrative produced when character, plot, and dialogue are combined, producing a particular effect, feeling, idea, or all three.
- Arc or throughline—the map of the journey a character makes through a story. It can be literal, or it can be figurative, marking the changes a character undergoes during the course of the action and providing dramatic and revealing moments.
- Conflict—the engine of drama, created when the opposing forces that make a story interesting square off.
- Objective—what the character needs and pursues at all times, resulting from the conflict the playwright creates.
- Moments—specific islands of import in the story's progression or arc; places in the script where moments can be made, revealed, and/ or portrayed dramatically. Victories, defeats, and discoveries are often made there.
- Physical actions—the things the actor does either by choice or because the script requires it to make thoughts and feelings clear.

As a result of our previous work, we have already accumulated a detailed set of given circumstances, outlined the story contained in the one-act play *Eye to Eye* by Christopher Graybill, and chronologically listed or *scored* the chronological cause-and-effect sequence of actions that make it up. Our examination in the last chapter was based on the premise that everything a playwright puts into his script is there for a reason, and our ability as actors to effectively use what is in that script will help us make choices– that are compelling to watch and that will help tell the story in the most effective way.

Now let's take a closer look at the actions contained in the story in the hopes of coming to appreciate how those actions are painstaking laid out by the playwright, not unlike railroad tracks that will take us to a predetermined destination—a destination that will make the story work. When we follow the railroad tracks the playwright has laid down, we are much more likely to serve both the story and ourselves than if we simply followed our own path.

In this chapter, we will focus on the conflict found in the play and figure out its relationship to objective playing. We will then analyze the script for possible objectives to play, and we'll apply those chosen objectives to the script directly. Ultimately, we want to be able to divide the play into beats, using objectives and tactics. This will allow us to effectively score the story contained in the script and reveal who the characters are—through the actions we choose to play and how we play them.

In spite of the work we did in the previous chapter, your understanding of the machinery of the action is still missing an important ingredient. This ingredient is the catalyst that will ensure the story you tell will be a good one. What I am talking about here is *conflict*—often referred to as the engine of drama. The action of any play centers around its conflict, and the playwright writes his story keeping this in mind. The conflict invariably forces the characters in that story to choose a course of action intended to resolve the conflict, and the conflict will continue to fuel the action until it is finally resolved. In most stories, the main conflict comes from the well-placed opposition of characters who somehow stand in each other's way.

Keeping in mind that the basic conflicts possible in a story include person versus person, person versus himself (internal conflict), or, in rarer cases, person versus nature, see if you can determine the answers to the following questions:

- What conflicts are found in the play *Eye to Eye*?
- Which of these conflict is/are most important? Why and how?
- What is/are the connections between the conflicts in the story and its two primary characters? The third minor character? How do these conflicts essentially generate the action of the play?

The action in *Eye to Eye* has one central conflict from which all the action originates. At first a courting dance seems to be enacted, but once the woman asks for the check, the central conflict concerns that check and who will pay it. For both the man and the woman, the act of paying the check makes a statement regarding their relationship. For the man, it suggests that the woman has been impressed enough with him to allow him to pay. For the woman, paying the check frees her from the obligation of further contact with the man. The playwright has more in mind than check paying, however, and the conflict is more about the nature of men and women and how they relate to each other. But in terms of the story's action, the battle for the check provides the engine of drama.

Again, as with so much of the analysis process, there are no absolute correct answers; there are only answers that work best to tell the story of the play and your character. Each of the characters might be said to have both internal and person-versus-person conflicts. Both are driven in part by their attitudes toward and about the opposite sex, and their own internal conflicts regarding the opposite sex no doubt fuel their emotions and, in turn, their responses. But in terms of the play, winning the right to pay the bill generates the action and the sparks.

At the outset, the man tries to win the woman over. Perhaps he is trying to seduce her. In the opening chat, he reaches for the woman, stares into her eyes, and tries to draw compliments from her. He accepts negative responses from her and lightly attempts to charm her in return. He uses his wit, his sense of humor, and his sexuality as tools to succeed with her. He powers his way with her and tries to control the conversation in order to control her. For her part, the woman plays defense, boxing her way out of trouble by taking the man literally when she knows he's joking, by using veiled hostility hidden in witty repartee, and by honestly declaring to him that he makes her uncomfortable. But when the waiter comes, the woman asks for the check and the major conflict begins.

From that point on, the play becomes a tactical war in which the two central characters try to win the check and the right to pay it. The tactics range from juvenile to nasty, from physical to intellectual to emotional. Only the waiter's interruptions slow down the ongoing contest—a contest that continues to play out even past the woman's exit. The playwright has implied a variety of smaller objectives or *tactics* that each of the lead characters can use on each other. It will be up to the actors to find those tactics and show the audience when each of the tactics succeeds or fails. It will also be the actors' responsibility to make clear the transition from one tactic to the next as a necessary result of observing their moment-by-moment victories and defeats.

The actor playing the waiter must also have an objective to play. Like the lead characters, that objective must be simple, clear, and important. But it must always serve the story, not get in its way. What does the waiter want?

OBJECTIVE PLAYING — TOOL NUMBER ONE

How can he go about getting it in an interesting way without making the story about him? That is always the trick in playing supporting characters.

Notice how talking about conflict automatically leads to a discussion of *objective*. Just in case you are still fuzzy about the term, an objective (also referred to as *intention, need, want, goal, action,* etc.) is the prize an actor as character must pursue at all times. Unlike in life, where we often carry out actions without realizing why we do so, an actor must make choices for his character even when his character may not consciously be doing so. By playing a specific objective, and constantly using strategy to achieve that objective, the actor as character is able to find effective choices and commit to them. This choosing process allows the actor to avoid random actions that do not contribute to the story. The strong choices that result from playing objectives will reliably serve the story. Since any story is based on conflict, and an actor's objective pitted against an opposing force makes up that conflict, it follows that by playing an objective at all times, the actor will serve the needs of the script.

If you accept this analysis, then you are ready to go back to the script and examine it even more specifically. Keep in mind that the objectives I noted refer to the overall objectives of the two lead characters, but the tactics to be used must be defined very specifically. The more specifically you can define the tactics, the more specific your work is likely to become, and the more colors you will be able to show in your character. If you've ever heard a performance described as one-level, this description usually means that the actor has stuck to a single choice for smaller objectives or tactics, or played generalized ideas rather than specific and clearly defined tactics. This error usually results in the making of one-dimensional characters.

It is important to note that what we are doing here is homework, and subject to change when you start rehearsing. Ultimately, your ideas about the play and how to do it will have to merge with those of the other actors and the director. But for now your job is to arm yourself with the clearest and most exciting choices you can make — choices that are consistent with and support the story that is unfolding. If that is what you bring to the table when rehearsals actually start, you will be doing the job that is expected of you, and you will be doing the kind of job that generates creativity and excitement.

In *Eye to Eye* the man is the more aggressive main character. He often initiates the action, both physical and psychological. In other words, he is the one who usually does things first physically, and he is the one who usually starts a new objective or tactic. As stated earlier, the woman, at least until the climax is reached, spends more time reacting to the ploys of the man. But many times her reactions end up as wins, forcing the man to rethink his moves and come up with new ones when previous ones fail. It will be up to the actors to find those wins and losses in the script and figure out how to play them. It will also be their responsibilities to come up with the new tactics following those moments of victory and defeat.

At many moments in the rehearsal process, new information is put on the table and new discoveries are made by each of the characters. These discoveries are usually about another character. The new information often causes each of the characters to come up with new tactics as a result of what they have learned. How does the man in *Eye to Eye* react, for instance, when the woman tells him that the looks he gives her are too intimate? Deciding his reaction helps tell the story and shows character. What should the actor be showing? Or how should the woman react when the man tells her that her eyes are very beautiful, or that she will have to compete in a staring contest if she wants to pay the bill? Should choices like this be left to the spontaneity of the moment only? As an actor, you are the storyteller. Do you want to leave it all to chance later in rehearsal?

It is also the actors' responsibility to justify the actions stated in the stage directions and implied by the characters' dialogue. Why, for instance, is the man reaching for the woman at the top of the play? The actor must justify that action and play it in an appropriate manner—in a manner that reveals character and forwards the story. Why do the stage direction say that the man reaches for her hand but does not touch it? Does he stop himself? Or does he stop because of the woman? What does the woman do that causes him to stop? Is it a look? Does she pull her hand away? Something else? There is no explanation in the script, but if you follow the stage directions—and unless you have a very good reason to ignore them, you should follow them—you will have to provide the reason through your actions.

All right, now you are ready to return to the script and see how many objectives and/or *tactics* (specific ways of achieving your larger objective) you can identify. What tactics does man use, and where? Where and why do these tactics change? Where specifically is the woman confused or defeated by the man's tactical moves? Where does her response produce victories for her? Defeats? With all this in mind, go back to the script and mark possible objectives that each of the characters will be playing and note where they occur. Also note where all objectives and tactics change. In other words, where do the *transitions* occur? Draw a line after the last line of an objective, just at the spot where the change to a new objective or tactic happens. Then write in the new objective or tactic right below that line. This will help you recognize that you have indeed come to the end of a *beat,* and it will remind you to begin playing the new one you have marked in. When you have done so, we'll go into a little more detail.

If you followed the instructions, you succeeded in finding where the *beats* of the play change. A *beat* is the term given to the length of script during which an actor plays a particular objective or tactic. When an actor changes from one objective to another, it is called a *transition.* Remember, a beat ends when an objective is won or lost, when new information is introduced that will change the character's need, when a discovery is made that changes the character's need, or when there is an interruption imposed by outside forces that must be dealt with (each time the waiter arrives, for instance). Whenever a beat ends, for any one of these reasons, it is the actor's job to transition from one beat to another clearly and believably. Sometimes this can be done without fanfare; other times it is necessary to for the actor as character to show how and why this change happens. Keep in mind that these transitions from one objective to another are likely to create powerful moments onstage if you are able to shape them fully and clearly.

There are no right or wrong answers, but your goal is to tell the story of the play and your character as clearly and as compellingly as you can. Here is a partial list of smaller objectives or tactics the actor playing the man might use in his "seduction" of the woman in the first section of the play.

To make her feel wanted.

To make her feel wrong.

To make her feel like she is unfairly accusing.

To make her feel sexually attractive.

To make her confess intimate things about herself.

To challenge her viewpoint.

To make her feel silly.

To make her confess intimate things about herself.

To make her feel safe about being intimate.

To make her think he's charming.

To make her think she's fascinating.

Do any of the tactics listed above match some that you came up with? See if you can find where these tactics could be played in the script. Remember, each choice of tactic will affect the way the story unfolds and how the audience perceives that story and its characters. Each cumulative choice will affect the manner in which the story moves forward and give more information about the characters to the audience. You are responsible for creating an effective library of information — information that helps tell the story effectively and that tells the audience things about your character that will make the story work the way it should. That is your job.

In the first beats of *Eye to Eye,* for instance, the man tries a series of tactics, all intended to win over his date for the evening. Whether he is ultimately trying to seduce her, simply win a second date, or something in between is never made clear in the script, so it becomes entirely up to the actor playing the role. But clearly, the man is unrelenting in his pursuit. Tactically he tries a variety of things to win the woman over. He seems almost unstoppable, smoothly turning from one tactic to the next until the waiter finally interrupts their ongoing battle. When the woman abruptly asks for the check, it is a big news item for the man. You can put this moment under the category of *discovery* or *new information,* but whatever you choose to call it, it is definitely a beat ender. For all three characters, her request for the check becomes a transitional moment — and when it is over, each of the characters will be pursuing a new objective. For the man and woman the new objectives becomes the right and privilege of paying for the check. For the waiter, the objective is now to complete the transaction in a way that will get him the biggest possible tip.

How the man plays his opening objective and tactics will start to define him for the audience. How, specifically, the woman responds to his tactics will begin to define her. Audiences cannot see into the hearts and minds of characters on stage. They can only see what characters do and how they do it. That means that your choices as an actor carry a great deal of importance. Dialogue can be said in a multitude of ways. The tactics you select to play will influence how you say that dialogue. But the tactics you select will also influence what you do physically and how you do it.

Let's go back to the opening moments once again for some examples of what I'm talking about. As the lights come up, how should the man be positioned in relation to the woman physically? Does where the characters sit and how they are sitting influence how the story will be perceived by the audience? Position them in your heads in various ways, and then answer the question for yourself. Earlier I asked what the man's objective was in extending his hand toward the woman. The actor playing the man must know this. But the actor must also know how the man reaches for the woman. Is the movement aggressive and quick? Is it slow and sensuous? Something else? What is he trying to accomplish here, and what is the most likely way of doing it if the gesture is to be successful? How should the woman react? With a deliberate pull-away, or with a subtle retreat of her arm? What would each of her possible reactive gestures mean to the man, to the audience? What tells the best story of the moment and serves the script? What tells the best, most useful character information? All these questions are worth considering, and each reinforces the idea that playing objectives has both its psychological and physical components.

Keep in mind that all actions have beginnings, middles, and ends, and for the actor playing the man, reaching out toward the woman begins not with the action itself, but with the decision to do so. If the actor takes himself through the decision-making process, in this case, as the lights are coming up, that process will inform and affect the manner in which he actually extends his arm. Further, if he can somehow demonstrate his thinking process to the audience (assuming that he is visible to them) by what he does physically, then the actor is telling the story in the best possible way. The woman, on the other hand, will no doubt have a reaction when the man reaches for her. The same kind of questions to be answered would apply to the actor playing the woman.

There is another important storytelling issue here that has been hinted at in the preceding paragraphs. What should the audience be thinking and feeling about the man and the woman? Should the audience like these characters? Or is the man a creep? Maybe you think the woman is too uptight and poisoned by sexual politics? Or maybe they are both unlikable? Which is it? Is there only one answer? The truth is there is never only one answer. The answer you want to find is the one that will allow the play to work best.

Before you can answer any questions about how the audience should feel about the characters, you will have to go back to the story of the play and what you think the playwright's intent is. You might assume that since this play is about gender politics, we should not like the man. Men are always creepier in the sexual-politics war. Besides, in the end he does seem pretty nasty, so maybe the audience should not like him from the beginning. But does that really tell the story in the best possible way? What if we like the man at first and are totally charmed by him? Might not that give the ending a surprising punch and lend a more interesting arc to his character? Wouldn't his likeability give the woman more internal conflict to work with during their tactical war? These are only questions for consideration, and no two actors are likely to come up with the same answers. But issues like those raised here need to be considered, because your answer will affect the kind of choices you make regarding objectives and tactics.

Not every answer needs to be arrived at during your script analysis, by the way. In fact, much more will be learned in your active rehearsal process, but the more you explore your obligations to the story at the outset, the more prepared you will be to find in-the-moment answers later as you rehearse. Keep in mind that an actor who comes to rehearsal with no clue is far more likely to be unavailable for inspiration than one who is prepared. The clueless actor is nervous and busy dealing with himself. He is likely to be less available for responding in the moment; the actor who has done his homework and is confidently relaxed is much more likely to be focused outside himself and ready to respond to input. And this is often where the acting alchemy will happen.

Now that we have discussed the play a bit, you might want to go back to your notations to see whether the objectives and tactics you have put there are really specific enough, and whether they best serve the unfolding story and characters. Look very closely to see if each objective and tactic has its fulfillment, whenever possible, in the other character. An objective that has its completion in another character guarantees that there will be conflict to overcome. In other words, the man should really be targeting the woman, and the woman should really be targeting the man. Objective phrases structured as "to make someone do something" or "to keep someone from doing something" can be particularly effective for targeting the other character. It forces a connection between objective and target.

Remember, a playwright creates conflict whenever possible between characters—moment by moment and scene by scene—because she wants the story to be as gripping as possible. When an actor finds an objective that has its fulfillment in another character, you can be sure that the other character will somehow provide an obstacle to fulfilling that objective. It is up to you to hunt down these obstacles so that you can use them in your work effectively. In *Eye to Eye,* the characters have a good deal of internal conflict, as well. It would be your job as the actor playing the woman, for instance, to find the conflict and obstacles that exist within her and use them to color her choices of tactics and her playing of them as she deals with the man.

If you have carefully gone through the analysis process with me in this chapter and in the previous one, you should have a fairly clear understanding of the storytelling mechanism of *Eye to Eye* and its individual gears. You have a pretty good idea of who the characters are, what they need, and what's keeping them from getting it. You know the conflicts found in the story and the arc of the story as the man and the woman move toward fulfilling their objectives. You also have a good idea of the storytelling moments found in the play and the kind of choices you will have to make to shine maximum dramatic light on those moments.

During the rehearsal process you will deepen your understanding and make adjustments—in accordance with the modified story created when your choices are merged with those of the other actors and your director. You will have to give up some of your choices in order to create a uniform shared vision. Since theater is collaborative and developmental, nothing you have created in your homework process should be considered anything but a starting point. The understanding you will be bringing to the table, however, ensures that the time you spend in rehearsal will be productive and enlightened. If you are able to do this, you will have done the kind of homework expected of a professional.

In the next chapter, we will take a closer look at objectives—how to find them, and how they can help you define the story and make clear your character.

CHAPTER

NINE

M_ORE ON OBJECTIVES

WHEN DONE RIGHT, ACTING IN A REALISTIC PLAY OR MOVIE looks just like life. In fact, I often tell my students that if someone were looking and listening through the window on the door, they shouldn't be able to tell whether you're acting or not. Ultimately, when done well, acting looks easy. From the outside, it looks like doing what you do. But in reality, it's anything but.

Any civilian who has ever done an improv game and was then asked to read from a script knows just what I'm talking about. Maybe some of you do, too. When all you have to do is make it up on the spot and listen and react a little — no problem. If you're a cool dude and know how to relax and aren't too self-conscious, you can get lots of laughs and plenty of slaps on the back. But it's a whole different ball game when you're supposed to listen and react yet have the obligation to say a specific bunch of lines, move and do a specific set of things, and remember that the sum total of all you say and do is supposed to add up to the story you're trying to tell. No wonder so many actors find it a lot harder than it looks.

But even for those of us who can juggle all those balls at once, there is still more. If we're listening in the moment and reacting, how do we know what the right reaction is? And how do we know what to do next after we react? And if acting is supposed to be spontaneous, how can we be spontaneous and at the same time keep on the track set down in the script and worked on in rehearsal? And when and if we do something new and in the moment, how do we make sure that we don't head down a road we didn't intend on going down, especially if it takes us in a direction that doesn't serve the story or our characters?

These are tough questions, and until the turn to the twentieth century, when Stanislavski came up with his system, few actors, even the good ones, had tangible answers to offer each other. Actors mostly came up with their own ways of doing things based on observing veteran actors they respected, and by trial and error. Most actors learned their craft by the seat of their pants. When playwrights turned toward realism in the latter part of the nineteenth century, it sparked the search for a realistic way of acting that has continued on through today. And whether we approach acting through emotion or through action, or through some combination of the two, as actors we are always charged first and foremost with communicating the story in a believable manner.

Today most actors agree — whether their approach is emotion-based (Stanislavski's early exploration of craft) or action-based (his later approach) — that playing objectives is a key tool in their craft. Since actors are charged with telling the story the playwright sets out, all of their acting choices must ultimately do just that. In previous chapters, we have explored many of the ways to find and develop the story. First we will review what we have already learned about objectives up to this point, and then we will take a closer look at one of the most important of acting tools.

Because this has been a central theme of the book thus far, suffice it to say that stories are primarily based on, and develop around, conflict. *Conflict* can be defined as the opposition of two counterforces trying to defeat each other. The plot of any story begins to rise when a conflict develops. That conflict is most often between a story's central characters, and it builds until these characters confront each other at the story's climax, at which point the conflict begins to resolve.

There are three basic kinds of conflict: person versus nature, person versus himself, and person versus person (sometimes person versus society is also included). Some movies and novels revolve around a person-versus-nature (or -society) conflict — any survival story, for instance — but in theatre, person versus person is usually the dominant conflict, with aspects of person versus self often present. Stanislavski realized that if an actor is to fulfill her character's obligation to the unfolding drama, she must focus primarily on her part in the conflict. That means that the actor must identify what her character is trying to win overall in the story (he called this the *superobjective*), and more specifically what her character needs in a particular scene from the character or characters she shares the stage with (he called this the *objective*). In other words, Stanislavski determined that actors playing characters should focus exclusively on their characters' objectives and find *actions* to play (the things they do physically and verbally) that will move their characters toward those objectives.

This is all a big chunk to swallow, so let's break it down some.

Essentially Stanislavski was saying that acting, if you're going to do it effectively, must be simpler than life. In life, we don't always know what we're doing. We often respond emotionally or intuitively to the things that confront us moment by moment. Often these spontaneous choices are ill-advised or lead to dead ends, though sometimes they do miraculously lead to that pot of gold at the rainbow's end. More often than not, however, in life, even when the outcome is good, it is simply a matter of luck. But when you're acting in a play, you're telling a story that is essentially preset by the script. The words and actions set down by the playwright are the trail of breadcrumbs that you must follow. Otherwise the story won't get told at all, or certainly won't get told properly.

So acting is simpler than life in that as an actor playing a character, you must determine what your character needs and pursue it, no matter what. As we saw in the previous two chapters, you can find your character's objective (need, intention, goal, action, want, etc.) by first determining what the conflict of the story is and then by finding your character's part in that conflict. In other words, the conflict tells you what the fight is about, and from that you can determine what your character needs that will help make that conflict work. Once you know what your character needs, you, as the actor, must pursue getting that need fulfilled at all times. Notice that I said that you "as the *actor* must pursue..."

Here's the trick. Human beings in life are not always aware of what they need, and certainly even those who do know what they need don't necessarily pursue these needs at every moment. And, unlike actors playing a role, they don't know the outcome of their story. Characters in a play don't know their outcomes, either. But the actors playing them do. So, the actors playing those characters have the obligation to make choices for their characters based on the storyline that, unlike life, is preset. We know things even when our characters don't.

At every moment of a play, an infinite number of choices can be made, but only a certain number will lead down the path the script has laid out. As actors, we need to make choices that our characters could make, or might make, but the choices have to be ones that make the story work. Stanislavski realized that if an actor makes choices based on a character's needs, even when the character himself is not necessarily aware of those needs, the resulting choices will make sense, serve the script, and be interesting. This happens because the story's built-in conflict—often called the engine of drama—will be maintained and even fueled.

The amazing thing here is that even though you as the actor are making choices at all times intended to fulfill your character's objectives, the audience won't necessarily recognize that fact. You will still create the illusion that your character is a believable human being behaving just as human beings behave in life. The reason for this is that the audience sees the action of the play in the context of its totality. They make inferences and deductions about the whole play and all the characters in it. They fill in details and add complexity that you as your character can't see and need not be responsible for. In other words, as an actor playing a character, you can't do everything. But you must do the things the unfolding story requires of you. And you must not do things that go against the story the playwright has provided. Playing your objective will ensure that all this happens.

Here's an example of how this all works. Say you're a major league pitcher, a reliever; it's the ninth inning and you've just gotten the word to warm up because the starting pitcher has walked two men in a row. You get up and tug at your shirt a few times, not even aware you're doing so. Then you stare at the ground for a moment. After that, you start to throw some warm-up pitches, tentatively. The camera has been on you while you do this, and the announcers in the booth begin to comment on the fact that you look nervous but determined. As you continue to throw your warm-ups, you think about nothing but winning the game. The announcers in the booth note the way you pull at your pants, spit between pitches, and seem to not be throwing at full velocity. These actions cause them to continue to infer about your state of being from what they see you doing. In short, they describe a whole layer of subtext that you're not even thinking about, based on what they know about you, your history, the game, and the specific situation. It may not even be true, but it's what they perceive to be true. This is what an audience will do as they watch your actions onstage. They will add lots of detail based on what they know about your character, the given circumstances, and the story thus far.

As the pitcher, you continue to focus on your objective—saving or winning the game. You think about nothing else. When you get called in, your concentration becomes even more intense. In order to win, you will strategize about pitches, location, and how to handle each individual batter. Your overall objective stays the same, but you change your tactics according to who's at the plate. Even though what you do is totally concentrated, those watching you will impose all kinds of things onto the simple actions you perform. After the game, you'll be asked about all kinds of things that never even crossed your mind, and the reporters covering you won't believe you when you deny that these things were going on. This, too, is what an audience does, so playing a simple objective will be more than enough to provide your audience with complexity.

As you can see, a sporting event is a great metaphor for an acting situation—because your objective in a game is always literally to win, and you focus on your objective at every moment. Winning, for a committed athlete, is always the be-all and end-all. Anything that stands in the way of winning is an obstacle to be overcome. In an acting situation you should be trying to win at all times, as well—you're trying to win your objective. If as an actor you commit totally to winning your objective, if you make it as important to you as an athlete makes winning a game, you will be raising the *stakes* of the story so high that you will have to be interesting and, in turn, so will the story. The playwright will provide obstacles along the way—obstacles that you must overcome, or die trying. The actors you confront onstage will also be trying to win, and their choices will conflict with yours. What they do to get what they want may provide further obstacles to your getting what you want. You will have to confront their conflicting objectives and the obstacles they provide. You will have to employ *tactics* to get around their opposition. All of this will be in the script or provided by the other actors as a result of the choices they bring to the stage.

The more you are willing to *risk* to get what you need, the more interesting you will be. Now, don't get me wrong. You can't do things that won't be believed or that are inconsistent with the story or your character. (Everything you do onstage must be justified by the story—it must be consistent with and/or add to what is set down in the script.) The playwright, if she's a good one, has written a compelling play and has provided enough background and given circumstances that will allow you to make your choices as your character equally compelling. If you are acting with other actors who know their craft, they will also provide you with the opposition and obstacles you need to make your work exciting. It is your job to see that you rise to the occasion. The best way to do that is by going after what you need with all you've got.

Obtaining your objective as an actor playing a character is not always a straight or direct route, however. Sometimes you have to accomplish a sequence of smaller things in order to make that bigger objective happen. Here's an example. Let's say that Dorothy's superobjective is to get back home to Kansas. Fine. But first she has to find out how she can get back there. Glinda tells her she must locate the Wizard of Oz, who might know how to help. Dorothy's objective becomes to get to the Emerald City. Many obstacles stand in her way. Some of those obstacles she defeats, some she evades. Some come in the form of enemies who are out to get her, and some come in the form of natural obstacles like climate and geography. When she finally reaches the Emerald City, she has completed her objective. But it will immediately be replaced with a new one. Now she must find a way to get in to see the wizard. She will use a series of *tactics* (smaller strategies used to fulfill an objective) before she eventually gets in to see him, thereby completing another objective.

But the wizard also has his superobjective—to maintain the illusion that he is all-powerful. He also has an objective regarding Dorothy—to make her go away. And he uses a series of tactics to fulfill his objective, including to avoid seeing her. When Dorothy finally wins her objective and gets in to see him, the wizard, in trying to maintain his superobjective, finds a new objective. He orders Dorothy to bring back the witch's broom before he will satisfy her need. Since he is sure she will not be able to fulfill his command, he finds a way to avoid showing that he is not all-powerful—maintaining his superobjective.

Dorothy's new objective becomes to get that broom. She does this because it is a necessary detour that will, in the end, help her win her superobjective—getting back to Kansas. All of these smaller objectives become obstacles for her to overcome in order for her to get what she really needs. This is the essential story of *The Wizard of Oz*, and, interestingly, as the audience watches how Dorothy responds to the obstacles standing in her way while pursuing her objectives, they come to learn more and more about her in spite of the fact that the actor never wavers from playing what she needs. Her tactical choices and the manner in which she carries them out suggest plenty of character nuance in spite of the simple line of action that Judy Garland as the actor has to play.

Granted, the plotline of *The Wizard of Oz* is simple and the characters are straightforward, but even in character plays as subtle and complex as those by Chekhov or Tennessee Williams, it remains your job to find the conflict, determine the overall objective, and then recognize the smaller conflicts and objectives to play. Your character's superobjective in the script is usually the hardest to decipher. Sometimes it will be necessary to look for your objectives scene by scene before you are able to determine your overall superobjective.

Whether you find your superobjective first or last, you will always want to examine your objectives scene by scene, beat by beat, and moment by moment. The tactics you use to get your objectives and how you carry out these tactics will create a mosaic of actions that together will define your character for the audience. After all, you are what you do. Finding your objectives and staying on task at every moment is one of the most difficult acting disciplines to learn and to maintain. It takes much patience and practice to master this skill. But you must not try to avoid the obligation.

So, let's summarize a bit. Your character's superobjective—the objective for the whole play—does not change. You determine your suberobjective through careful study of the whole play. Whatever you select must ultimately be sustainable through the course of the entire unfolding drama. But smaller objectives do change. Like Dorothy, you must pursue your objective until it is won or lost, or until you give it up because of some new circumstance that arises—a new obstacle, information that changes your needs, or some other more immediate conflict. When an objective is won or lost, you must replace it with a new objective, and when some new circumstance arises that requires your commitment, your objective must transfer to that new situation. Remember, in order to pursue your superobjective it sometimes becomes necessary to handle the immediate problem before getting back to the bigger goal.

Sometimes, when trying to figure out your objective in a scene, it helps to narrow down your choices somewhat. By breaking down possible objectives that can be played into categories, you may find it easier to figure out exactly what you need and the ways to get it. Here again are those six basic categories of objectives mentioned earlier in the book. I'm sure there are other ways to categorize, but this breakdown has been very helpful to me and my students over the years. It offers logic and simplicity.

To give information

To get information

To make someone feel good

To make someone feel bad

To make someone do something

To keep someone from doing something

To give information is the most simplistic and dullest objective. You can fulfill this objective simply by giving the information you are supposed to give. Unless you find a way to spice it up, this objective really should be just a place holder—until you find a stronger, more specific, and more challenging objective. To give information becomes interesting only if there is an obstacle in the way of delivery. If, for instance, you are a messenger in a Greek play and the information you must give has the potential to make the king receiving the information angry or upset, then your objective becomes to give the information without getting killed. In other words, how can you avoid the "kill the messenger" syndrome? That is far more interesting. It raises the stakes and forces you to risk. Ultimately, you always want to find an objective with maximum storytelling potential. If your job onstage is to give information, try to find an obstacle that will give you more to do and make what you do more interesting.

To get information, on the other hand, can be a tactical cornucopia. If you're trying to get information, the script itself will probably provide you and your scene partner with plenty of raw material to mine. If you're trying to get info, then the character from whom you're trying to get this information will probably not want to share it, or knows that to share will be dangerous. The step-by-step revealing of information will likely be so fraught with new and interesting stuff that there will be plenty to react to as the scene progresses.

If the character in opposition to you doesn't want to reveal information, you will have to employ many tactics to extract it. You can likely employ an entire arc of tactics ranging from flattery to threat. You will have to look closely at the script, as well as play off of your scene partner's reactions, to find what works and what doesn't. You will probably have to go through a series of losses before the info is completely revealed — if it is revealed. Or you will collect the info bit by bit and have a lot of new info revealed piecemeal and will be able to react to it. In the end, the script will determine whether you are successful or not. As the actor, you know this; as the character, you do not. You will make choices for your character that serve the script and proceed moment to moment as if you do not know the outcome.

Making someone feel good or bad is a straightforward, easy objective to start with. That means using the dialogue and everything else available to you to do just that. How you use the space, proximity to your scene partner, physical contact, the set and props, and so on can all help you fulfill your objective. The hardest thing about this meta-objective for beginning actors is to stay on task. Often actors feel they are not offering up enough colors or dimension of character when they adhere to a single objective, and they allow themselves to drift on to something else. Invariably, this drifting weakens and muddies the scene the playwright has provided.

Most of the time the scene will be written in such a way that you will be forced to change tactics anyway. You must always *justify* the dialogue you have to say by making choices that are consistent with the story as written. So shifting as the dialogue indicates will give you the opportunity to show a variety of colors. But remember, you never have to do the whole play when you're doing a scene. If you think your character is being too nice or too mean in a particular scene, the rest of the play will inevitably dilute or change this impression. People do not act with consistency at every moment in life. Even *nice* people under certain circumstances show a darker side. The good playwright takes care of this problem when she writes the script. An individual scene is only about a few of the mosaic tiles that make up the larger picture of the story and your character. You must do what you need to, and do it fully, when required. That means play your objective fully. Trust the tracks the playwright has laid down.

To make someone do something or to keep someone from doing something will cover all other situations. In fact, these two meta-objectives are really all the objectives you'll need. All actions that you might want to play can be made to fall into these categories, and to do so will ensure that you pursue those actions with vigor. Essentially, in any given scene where you are onstage with another character, you should always be trying to make that other someone do something. The very nature of the phrase *to make someone* _____ suggests a strength, urgency, and commitment to the task at hand that you will always want to bring to your work. It suggests a willingness to risk and to focus on the other characters you share your scene with. Since your job is to make the story as compelling as possible, thinking in terms of making someone do something puts you right in the zone.

Since most conflicts onstage involve person-versus-person clashes, shaping your objective into a *to make someone do something* goal, by nature of semantics, requires that your objective must be fulfilled through your scene partner. Framing your objective as *to make someone do something* will keep your moment-to-moment work focused on your target and remind you that you're playing your objective at all times. As a result, you and your scene partners will be strongly connected and likely to react to each other. (Transitive verbs—verbs that have receivers, for those of you who stayed awake during grammar lessons—are also useful in objectives and particularly useful for defining tactics. We will go into that a bit more later.) Sometimes the playwright also writes in a person-versus-self conflict that can function as an obstacle standing in the way of completing your person-versus-person objective. Sometimes you will want to add an obstacle yourself. It will heighten the urgency of the scene. An example of that kind of obstacle is coming up.

In film, conflict is not limited by time, space, and budgets, so scripts don't have to depend on person-versus-person dynamics as much as onstage work does, but eventually the conflict will come down to that. The same principles of drama apply—just on a broader palette. Take, for example, the Bourne franchise. Jason Bourne wants *to make the assassin* he has just "subdued" *talk.* He needs to get information. As a tactic, he first *threatens,* "I will cause you more pain than you ever dreamed of." His enemy resists. Then Bourne *punishes*—he hits his enemy on the kneecaps with a bat. His enemy screams, and Bourne stops. For a moment, he thinks about his enemy's position, and he knows the two of them are more alike than different. An internal conflict has arisen for him—an obstacle to completing his objective. He pursues his objective anyway. He must. Bourne now *scares* his adversary by pulling out his gun and placing it against his temple. "I will kill you if I have to," he says intimately, reflecting his internal conflict. "St. Petersburg," the assassin tells him. Bourne has won his objective. He hits his adversary with the butt of his gun across the temple. And a new objective is begun.

An action-based film, like any one of the Bourne series, is ideal for examining objective playing. Literally, the script allows actor Matt Damon no time to do anything else. Study one or more film in this series as a student of acting. Chart the objective playing, starting with superobjective and working down through objectives and tactics. You will find the concept of playing objectives strikingly clear if you watch the movie with this framework in mind. Look for transitions from one objective to the next. You will observe victories, defeats, and new information that cause the characters to change their objectives and tactics. After the movie is over, see if you can articulate a description of Jason Bourne's character. You will probably be able to do so despite the film's nonstop action, brutality, and lack of time spent on character development. Damon's Bourne character comes through because of the actions played and the manner in which Damon carries those actions out.

One last point on objective playing—the concept of *playing the positive*. A positive objective is one that will get you what you need, even if it is a negative thing to do. In the Bourne example I cited, Damon does many ugly, unpleasant things to his adversary. But each of those tactics helps him toward getting his objective fulfilled. In terms of his need to get information, or, rather, to make his adversary give him that information—threatening, punishing, and scaring are all positive choices. They would have been negative choices had his objective been to make his adversary like him. You must always make positive choices onstage or when acting in film. Otherwise, you are not really playing your objective at all.

Here I will provide a list of verbs that might be used in formulating objectives. Some of the verbs suggest urgency far more than others. Those that do are the ones that will make you and your character interesting. Some of the verbs are very specific, others rather vague. Some don't necessarily involve a receiver. Try out some of these verbs as objectives with a partner. You can do it by improv or by applying these objectives to scenes you are familiar with or working on. Note which ones really give you something specific to go after onstage—something that clearly engages the person sharing the scene with you. Use only verbs that really allow you to target your receiver. You may find that using the phrase to make the other character _____ proves far more effective in making your work clear, compelling, and tangible. If the list proves helpful, by all means, use it. All acting craft should be about making your work as strong as possible through the simplest process possible. Use what works for you. Just keep in mind that passive verbs, or ones that do not actively target or involve the other actor sharing the stage with you, likely will not prove useful.

To:

absolve	berate
abuse	bewitch
accept	blame
acquaint	bluff
acquit	boost
address	brainwash
admonish	bribe
affront	cajole
aid	calculate
alarm	call
alert	catch
allow	caution
amaze	challenge
amuse	charge
anger	charm
antagonize	chastise
appeal	cheat
arouse	chide
assess	coax
assist	coddle
astound	coerce
attack	command
baby	commend
badger	con
baffle	conceal
bait	condemn
beckon	confide
beg	confirm
beguile	confound
belittle	confuse

contest	dramatize
convince	draw
correct	duck
corroborate	ease
court	educate
cover	elevate
criticize	elicit
crucify	enchant
crush	endear
curse	endure
damn	enflame
dare	engross
deceive	enlighten
defy	ensnare
delight	entangle
delude	entertain
demean	entice
denigrate	entrap
denounce	entrust
deny	eradicate
detect	estimate
deter	evade
devastate	evaluate
dictate	excuse
direct	execute
disconcert	exploit
discourage	facilitate
discredit	feed
disgrace	force
disgust	frame
dishearten	free
dispirit	frighten
displease	frustrate
distress	gag
divert	goad
dodge	harangue
dominate	hassle

help
humble
humiliate
humor
hurt
hypnotize
imitate
impair
implicate
indict
indoctrinate
induce
indulge
insinuate
inspire
insult
interview
invite
judge
lead
lecture
libel
liberate
lure
magnetize
malign
maneuver
manipulate
mask
mend
mimic
mislead
misuse
mortify
motivate
muffle
muster

mystify
nag
nauseate
negotiate
notify
nullify
obliterate
offend
oppose
organize
overlook
panic
parrot
patronize
perform
perplex
persecute
peruse
placate
plan
please
pledge
preoccupy
press
prevail
prick
prod
promise
promote
prompt
propel
propose
prosecute
provoke
pursue
quash
quench

rally	soothe
ratify	spoil
ravage	spur
rave	spurn
read	squash
rebuke	squelch
recreate	startle
rectify	still
reiterate	stir
reject	stretch
release	strike
remedy	strip
renege	study
repel	stymie
reprimand	substantiate
repulse	suffer
resist	suggest
retract	summon
revolt	support
ridicule	suppress
satisfy	surprise
scheme	swindle
scold	tantalize
scrutinize	tarnish
sedate	tease
seduce	tempt
settle	terrify
shake	thwart
shame	tickle
shroud	titillate
shun	tolerate
sicken	torment
simplify	torture
slander	trick
slur	trouble
smother	tyrannize
snare	unburden

understand	vindicate
urge	warn
vacillate	woo
validate	worry
verify	worship
victimize	wrangle

In the next chapter we'll take a look and a listen to that other essential element of acting that doesn't come from the script. But it is ultimately the one that will make you believable onstage. And without this element, no matter how well you mine the script, you'll still look like you're acting.

FINDING THE SMALLER NUGGETS

I JUST WANTED YOU TO KNOW THAT EVERYTHING I'VE SAID up to this point in the book is wrong.

Only kidding.

I was just trying to make a point. About making moments. The principal subject of this chapter. Related to a few other connected subjects. Like listening (see Chapter 11). And learning how to read a script effectively—the subject of this entire book. The cornerstone of all my teaching. (Please note the seemingly halting way this paragraph is written. It is intentional.)

I believe that most students can learn to act—if they are willing to think in terms of what they are *doing*. This means thinking in terms of the big picture painted in the script, as well as attending to moment-to-moment miniatures. For the most part, this book has concerned itself with the big-picture items. But in this chapter we will examine some smaller but, in their own way, equally important nuggets of acting gold.

Hopefully, by now you have bought into the premise of this book—that the only way you can figure out what you should do onstage or onscreen—independently, that is—is by learning to decipher your script. For most students of acting, unfortunately, script analysis is not a pleasant prospect. It is not sexy work in and of itself, and before you picked up this book you may have tried to avoid it as much as possible. But keep in mind that learning how to decipher a script effectively will have a big payoff for you. Actors armed with the skills that this kind of map reading provides can turn a seemingly dry enterprise into sexy and fun work during the next step of acting—the making-choices and executing part.

You have learned that actors who make choices based on the script are far more likely to make choices that are clear and compelling and that serve the story being told. Script analysis is craft. It takes a lot of practice to master, a conceit that musicians and committed athletes take for granted. Learning to play the piano takes practice. Learning to find the strike zone takes practice. So does learning how to read a script. And learning to recognize and effectively play the moments in a script may take a lot of practice, too.

By way of example, let's go back to the opening lines of this chapter. Those lines contain potentially two big moments. If you hadn't been reading the book up to this point, learning that all of the previous chapters were filled with incorrect information might have meant little to you. You would have had little stake in what I say and wouldn't have wasted many hours of your time. The news would have been a nonmoment, there would have been nothing to react to, and you'd have ice-skated right past it. In life, we're under no obligation to make what we do exciting, interesting, or clear to others. But actors telling stories have that obligation.

On the other hand, if you are a committed student of acting who shelled out money to buy this book, and your time is precious, you might have had a strong reaction to my announcement. And then another strong reaction to the news that I was only kidding. If you liked the previous chapters and found them useful, your spontaneous reaction might have been shock followed by a moment of sadness. If you were a new student of acting and had been excited by the premise of the book, both statements might have had a profound effect on you. In other words, the given circumstances of your situation would have made this news of major importance. So would the reprieve offered when I told you I was only kidding. Approaching from the opposite angle, if you were trained as a method actor and you rely on emotions for your reactions, you might have been disagreeing with everything up to that point in this book. In that case, you might have felt a moment of great satisfaction and sung a stream-of-consciousness aria when you read the first line. Your opinions had been validated.

If the announcement had caused any of the reactions described in the preceding paragraph, or any other *strong* reaction, for that matter, then that first line would have provided an interesting and actable moment had it been a line from an actual script. But if the given circumstances of the script suggested that you were unfamiliar with the earlier parts of the book, then you would have had no reaction, and the news would have been glossed over as a nonmoment.

Now, here's the point: when done well, acting in a realistic play seems like life, but the fact is, it is not. It is simpler than life—simpler because in life people behave in the moment without regard for storytelling. What we do from moment to moment does not necessarily connect to the big-picture story of our lives (though in hindsight it may seem so at times). But when actors act moment to moment, they tell the story of the play, a story that the playwright has painstakingly set down in cause-and-effect fashion. Moments are built into the story and must be acknowledged and dealt with. These moments are little stories with their own beginnings, middles, and ends, and they connect to the next piece of story that the playwright has provided.

Too often, actors are busy being believable, or feeling their feelings. They disregard the fact that, like it or not, they are being pulled along a predetermined road that will always end the same way. The good actor will make choices that clarify and enhance that story path. This means that all the stepping stones, including these little storytelling moments, need to be dealt with like the nuggets of gold they are. But when actors choose to ignore these moments or when they are blind to them, they imperil the story as well as their own character work.

Writers tell the story through dialogue and implied action. They tell about who the characters are by what they choose to have the characters say about themselves or about each other. They tell about who their characters are by the way they shape what their characters say and by how they say it. Take a moment now, if you will, and go back to the third paragraph of this chapter—the one right after "Only kidding." I intentionally shaped that paragraph in a particular way. It has a series of short, staccato sentences. When said aloud, it would force an actor to take each of those short sentences and deal with them individually and specifically. Had I used my usual longer sentence style, it would be far easier to gloss over the individual ideas presented in the paragraph. It would have weakened the story-making potential of the lines, and it would have minimized the moments suggested there. As a result, it would have allowed an actor as character to generalize about who he is and what he is doing when he says all this.

Take a moment and try reading that paragraph aloud. Pay attention to the way it is written, and use the way it is written to actively make moments. Try to find the arc in the paragraph.

By paying attention to the way the lines are individually constructed and to the structure of the lines together, you probably found an arc that built to a climax of sorts, and you probably discovered some individual moments that had their own beginnings, middles, and ends. You were able to do this either because you heard the music of the lines intuitively, or because my pointing these things out to you allowed for you to see and hear them.

Finding and making moments is something every good actor can do. Some do it intuitively because they listen and react effectively onstage. You can't learn intuition, but you can learn to listen and react. You must take every opportunity to do so. This skill can be improved through practice. Through repetition. But the other way of finding moments is by learning how to see them in the script. This, like all the other elements we have discussed previously, requires that you learn how to read a script effectively. As you know by now, this also takes practice and repetition.

Here, then, are some exercises on how to make moments through developing listening skills and by using the script.

EXERCISE 1 — LISTENING AND REACTING TO WRITTEN MATERIAL

Choose a piece of written material that you find interesting. Material that when read aloud lasts a minute or so will be plenty long. The material can be copy from a magazine ad, paragraphs from newspapers and periodicals, a short poem, a letter that has been lying around, an e-mail, song lyrics, whatever.

Prepare to read it as though you were going to have to read it in front of your acting class. If you are not a good reader, practice the simple reading of it enough times so that reading is not an issue or an obstacle. In other words, give it the kind of preparation that as an actor you should be making. Once you can read it smoothly, add in the other acting elements—things like finding and hitting operative words, making sure there is a dramatic arc, and playing an objective or objectives. You can figure out the details that will make this an effective read. Once you are satisfied with the reading you have done, record it.

And here is where the real focus of this exercise comes into play. The exercise is not really about you as the speaker. It is about how you as a listener respond to what you hear when you play it back. Try listening to what you have recorded in the following way:

Your job is to react to the material as you hear it. Anytime something important, interesting, newsworthy, funny, or notable is read, you should react. The reaction should be physical and vocal, but no actual words should be used. Your reactions need not be loud or disruptive, but you should make them as apparent and as specific as possible. You should not perform these reactions. They should be realistic and spontaneous. Consider the exercise to be not unlike what a congregation might do in response to a sermon. Or what an audience might do during a political speech. The more specific you make your individual reactions, the better. The exercise is intended to give you practice in identifying and responding to potential moments, and to experience their relation to listening and reacting. You may want to do the exercise several times so that you give yourself a chance to refine your responses by making them clearer and more effective. But don't be afraid to go with what happens in the moment. Ultimately, it is your job to sift through your reactions and build on them.

Here, for instance, is a cutting from a *Los Angeles Times* article that I picked up on the Internet.

Facing an outcry from Hillary Rodham Clinton and John McCain, Barack Obama expressed regret Saturday for saying that small-town Americans embittered by job losses cling to religion, guns and hostility toward immigrants to explain their frustrations.

Obama's move underscored the political damage wrought by his remark last weekend at a San Francisco fundraiser. Clinton, his rival for the Democratic presidential nomination, made it the focus of her campaign Saturday.

Trying to drive a wedge between Obama and working-class Democrats in states with upcoming primaries, Clinton's campaign also deployed an army of surrogates to echo her condemnation of the Illinois senator. Among them were the mayors of Scranton, Bethlehem and several other cities in Pennsylvania, where the Democratic contest is nine days away.

Campaigning in Indiana, Clinton said she "was taken aback by the demeaning remarks Sen. Obama made about people in small-town America."

"Sen. Obama's remarks are elitist and they are out of touch," she told a crowd in Indianapolis.

The New York senator went on to proclaim the importance of gun rights and religious faith. "Americans who believe in the 2nd Amendment believe it's a matter of constitutional rights," she said. "Americans who believe in God believe it is a matter of personal faith."

There are so many things in the extract above that could be reacted to, and the first time through, you could actually be reacting at every moment. But if you do, it will be overkill, and nothing will seem to have particular importance since everything does. If this turns out to be the case, play the recording again but simply listen and jot down the things that seem to be of most interest and of most moment-making potential. Then listen to the article one more time and react overtly only to the items you have decided are the *most* significant.

You can repeat this process as many times as it is productive to do so. But you should be defining and refining your responses physically and vocally each time the reading is repeated. Moments can be sharpened, intensified, and clarified by identifying and developing their beginnings, middles, and ends. By the time the exercise is over, by listening and crafting a series of responses, you should be defining, through your reactions, who you are and where the big moments in the script are located. In addition, you will be helping to create the overall story progression.

Here is a variation of the exercise that can help you in your character work. First define a set of given circumstances for the character you are playing. Then listen to the recording and respond in a way that is consistent with the given circumstances you have described. The given circumstances will and must affect the way you respond to the news story. For instance, a Hillary fan will support and respond positively to her attack on Obama. Obama supporters will respond negatively to her negative aggression. A working-class voter might take umbrage to Obama's perception of the way they think and just might feel a touch of elitism coming from those words. Gun supporters might react in a particular way. Religious people might react in another. You get the idea. The point is you will have an opportunity to not only practice listening, but practice listening and making moments defined by the given circumstances you bring to your listening.

Each selection you find and record will reveal its own challenges. If you are willing to spend the time on this kind of exercise, you can greatly improve your appreciation for and ability at listening and making moments. You can even build playlets from the selected material that will feature yourself as the reactive central character. You may want to collect the material that works best and keep it for future use. Who knows; you could end up with a watchable one-person show.

The ability to listen and react effectively is a wonderful talent and/or skill to possess, and a lot of theatrical magic can result from having it, but being prepared to tell the story effectively and dependably is greatly enhanced when you know what you have to do. Finding moments in the script beforehand is a good way to accomplish this. I sometimes refer to a *moment* as the smallest unit of story. Beat endings—when an objective is won, lost, or given up—almost always provide such moments. So does receiving new information or making a discovery. When these moments are found in the script, it is still up to you to find the appropriate response that reveals clearly what you as your character are thinking and feeling. This will be accomplished through what you do and say, and by the manner in which you do it and say it. You can work on these skills by using the same kind of material suggested in the first exercise.

Suppose you were to photocopy, for instance, the *Los Angeles Times* article reproduced earlier, read it carefully, and then circle any moment-making phrases you find in the text. You might get in the habit of doing this anytime you are reading. Looking at a variety of material in this way would quickly make you more sensitive to the script and to the potential for drama contained there. Following, you will find a second reprint of the *Times* chapter. The boldfaced phrases and sentences indicate my choices for potential reactive moments. If you select specific given circumstances, you can further narrow down the likely moment-making phrases and their significance.

Facing an outcry from Hillary Rodham Clinton and John McCain, **Barack Obama expressed regret** Saturday for saying that **small-town Americans embittered by job losses cling to religion, guns and hostility toward immigrants to explain their frustrations.**

Obama's move underscored the political damage wrought by his remark last weekend at a San Francisco fundraiser. **Clinton,** his rival for the Democratic presidential nomination, **made it the focus of her campaign Saturday.**

Trying to drive a wedge between Obama and working-class Democrats in states with upcoming primaries, Clinton's campaign also deployed an army of surrogates to echo her condemnation of the Illinois senator. Among them were the mayors of Scranton, Bethlehem and several other cities in Pennsylvania, **where the Democratic contest is nine days away.**

Campaigning in Indiana, **Clinton said she "was taken aback by the demeaning remarks Sen. Obama made about people in small-town America."**

"Sen. Obama's remarks are elitist and they are out of touch," she told a crowd in Indianapolis.

The New York senator went on to proclaim the importance of gun rights and religious faith. "Americans who believe in the 2nd Amendment believe it's a **matter of constitutional rights,"** she said. **"Americans who believe in God believe it is a matter of personal faith."**

The boldfaced phrases represent the places in the cutting with the most reactive potential for me. As I listened as an Obama supporter, those phrases would mean one thing; as I listened as a Clinton supporter they would mean quite another. As a blue-collar worker, as a gun-rights advocate, as a black man, as a soccer mom, some phrases might take on lesser or greater importance. The more you define your characters, the time, the place, and the location, the more your work can be sketched out and made specific.

Once the potential moments are found, you might want to try to convert their analysis to actions. If you choose to do so, you can follow the procedure described earlier in this chapter, or invent your own variations. Feel free to work from actual scripted material, as well, whenever you think you're ready or when it seems appropriate to do so.

Here's one more exercise. For this one you might want to conscript a partner to help you out. What you want to do is come up with a two-line moment-maker like the one found here:

I love you.

I love you, too.

As you can see, a moment-maker is a two-line sequence of dialogue that, when performed, automatically creates one or more strong acting moments. You can come up with these pairings on your own or, if you're working with a partner, start with a line you write down and have your partner respond in writing to it.

The simple two lines I provided potentially create several good moments: the moment of difficulty in trying to muster the guts to say the first line. The shared moment of hearing it. The moment of what it means for the two characters. You might also consider the whole sequence as a single moment with a beginning, middle, and end. It really doesn't matter how you break it down and define it, as long as the result is that the moment (or moments) is strong, clear, and specific and tells a story. Of course, true specificity will be reached only when you provide yourselves with given circumstances — that is, the who, what, when, and where, which form the context for saying the dialogue. This simple pair of sentences can keep you going for quite a while if the given circumstances continue to be manipulated. An infinite number of possibilities exist, depending on who the characters are, when and where the dialogue takes place, and the specifics of those characters' situation.

Next I will list some moment-makers that my freshman class came up with when I most recently did this exercise in class. Although these are not the most creative examples of dialogue I have ever seen, they still provide ammunition for a potentially wonderful series of moments.

You look kinda—
Yeah.

Wait a second; are you high?
. . . No.

I really like your shirt.
I really like your body.

I love you.
No, you don't.

Why are you here?
I live here, you idiot.

Where's my car?
I left it here last night.

Did you pick up the kids after practice?
Oh, crap . . .

You look like a slut in that dress.
I found it in your closet.

Did we . . . last night?
Yeah . . . oh, God.

How will I know?
You just will.

What if I can't?
I know you can.

I didn't do it.
How can I believe you?

Sometimes I...
I know...

Last night was incredible.
I know. I can't see you anymore.

Where were you last night?
At your boyfriend's house.

Does this dress make me look fat?
... No.

Then who *is* my real father?
Bruce Miller.

As innocuous, clichéd, or stupid as any of the two-liners above may seem, when you explore them closely you will see that they all share at least two good potential acting moments and set up the possibilities for good storytelling. Each pair is easy to memorize and can lend itself with little difficulty to simulating the dramatic situations found in scenework or a play rehearsal. Your job is to find and create the biggest, most compelling moment you can, while keeping it totally real. You should find as much detail as possible through the process of defining given circumstances. In turn, this will give you hints as to the actions, physical and psychological, you can use to tell the story.

By way of closing, I'd just like to say...

I am not your real father.
Whatever...

CHAPTER ELEVEN

ANALYSIS, ACTION, AND LISTENING FOR GOLD

EVEN WHEN WATCHING CLASSROOM SCENEWORK, IT'S pretty easy to tell which actors have equipped themselves to enter the marketplace and sustain a career. They're the ones who can bring their strong analysis skills to the scene and know how to make choices based on what they have learned from the script, yes; but these are the ones who can also listen as well as give and take onstage. As you have seen in the pages of this book, analysis and synthesis are essential for making choices about character and story action, but listening and reacting in the moment is every bit as important, and ultimately you must make all of these aspects work together. And that is the theme of this chapter.

By now you know that I believe analysis must be a central part of an actor's skills. It is an actor's job to interpret the script and make it work as much as it is the director's. Yet developing that ability, and the ability to convert good analysis into playable actions, doesn't get very much attention in most acting classes. These skills do not develop spontaneously. For that reason you will have to learn to master these skills on your own. It's true that this detective work is not as much fun as trust exercises or improv, but if you are willing to spend the time developing your voice and body, why aren't you willing to spend the time on your brain? As you have, hopefully, learned from this book, an essential part of developing your craft should involve learning to think like actors must.

The other day in my junior BFA acting class — a class that focuses on acting Shakespeare — two of my students put up a first read from *Julius Caesar.* They were working on the Brutus/Portia scene in act 2, in which Portia finds her husband still awake in the middle of the night. My students know that when they put up a first read of a scene I expect them to have analyzed it for all of its basics, including conflict, objective, given circumstances, relationship, story arc, and significant moments. I also expect them to be able to make choices, even in a reading, that sketch out the scene moment by moment. I also expect that scene partners will listen to each other and adjust their preconceived or previously rehearsed choices to whatever is going on from moment to moment during their read.

I think these are the same expectations that any casting director would have.

When doing a scene from Shakespeare, of course, there is also the added obligation of understanding the sometimes unfamiliar language and making choices vocally that ensure the meaning is delivered clearly and effectively. With Shakespeare, the language is primary, but if the scene is going to be rendered effectively, all of the nonlanguage issues I address must be considered, as well. After all, Shakespeare was not just a great poet; he was a consummate playwright who knew how to shape a scene dramatically. The guy knew how to tell a story.

My office happens to be located next to the studio where I hold my classes. I can hear everything that goes on out there if I choose to listen. Twenty minutes before class on the day in question, my Brutus entered the empty studio and began rehearsing for his scene. I could hear him repeating, line by line, phrase by phrase, every piece of his dialogue — in every conceivable way. What was he doing? He kept at it doggedly until the first members of his class invaded the space a few minutes before the session was to begin. I was curious about the process he was taking himself through. Was he trying to discover how to say his lines and act them by trial and error? Not a technique taught by me.

Since there were too many scenes going up that day and not enough time to spend working on them, I dispensed with the usual pre-scene discussion of *Julius Caesar* and asked only one question: "What is your objective in the scene?" The actor playing Portia said she "want[ed] Brutus to tell her what's wrong." I spent at least five minutes trying to get her to understand that "*making* Brutus tell her what's wrong" was a much better way to approach the action of the scene. It would give her a stronger objective to play and was well supported in the script. Trying to "*make* Brutus tell her" targets Brutus directly and turns her objective from a passive wish to an active choice, one in which she can use her scene partner actively. It would give her something stronger to do and would compel her to focus on her partner.

Wanting, on the other hand, requires no action. I can want something and do nothing about getting it. Making someone do something forces action and conflict, which is far more interesting to watch and to do. This is much more than a semantic game, by the way. Actors who make active choices focused on the other actors sharing the stage tend to be interesting, exciting, unpredictable, and eminently watchable. Actors who don't are much more likely to kill a scene. My Portia told me she got the point. Then I turned to Brutus and asked him.

"He wants Portia to leave," Brutus said.

After listening to me spend five minutes persuading the actor playing Portia that *making* is stronger than *wanting*, Brutus was still in the *wanting* mode. The rest of the class laughed in disbelief, and so did I. If you have trouble listening in life, how much more difficulty will you have when you are under the pressures of acting onstage?

The fact is that my juniors have been working on the concept of finding and playing strong objectives for more than two years, yet it is not that unusual for students to bring in a weak or irrelevant objective for their scene. My students are good actors, some of the best in the country, I believe, and in production they shine. In their third time up in class they shine. But many of them do not work willingly or effectively on their own, particularly when it comes to doing the basic things that can make them effective onstage.

Maybe you tend to be like this, as well, even after getting this far in the book. Over and over again, my students see how the application of craft helps them act more compellingly, yet they resist using that craft on their next scene assignment. Many students I work with want me to set up the structure for them, outline the scene for them, and show them the shape of what they need to do. This will not help them when they graduate, any more than it will help to practice saying lines in as many ways possible, as my Brutus did, hoping to stumble onto a choice that works.

To succeed in a professional audition, an actor must be prepared to make choices quickly and efficiently. The first read in acting class is a great deal like what actors do at auditions, and many of the students I work with do this badly. What an actor might be able to achieve ultimately is meaningless if she can't do it on her own when auditioning for that casting director.

The actual Portia/Brutus reading that my students brought in was no better than their articulation of objectives. The scene had no arc. There were no moments. I didn't understand the relationship between the characters. I don't think the fact that these two people care about each other ever crossed my actors' minds. If they had thought at all about the relationship between Portia and Brutus, they would have discovered the engine for developing the scene. If they had asked a few simple questions—What is the audience supposed to be seeing? What is the story we are telling? Who are these characters? What is their relationship to each other?—they might have then been able to make some choices that would have helped them better define the scene.

My actors didn't ask those questions, and as a consequence the scene was devoid of love, and nothing they said seemed to land. The scene had no dramatic progression. The characters were undefined. The actors were not listening to each other, and they failed to let any of the money moments happen. It was a flat scene that went forward because of the dialogue, not because the characters were going on a journey.

The scene failed because my actors had not yet learned to work independently, to analyze a script effectively, to make choices physically that read clearly, believably, and powerfully to an audience. But, and perhaps most importantly, they failed to listen and react to their scene partner moment by moment, which would have given their work the seeming spontaneity that real-life behavior has. This is what actors who get jobs can do.

In the pages of this book you have already learned many craft elements that you can employ to make your work believable, reliable, and compelling. Employing these concepts will help you develop the important craft habits that you will need if you are to successfully work independently. Let's examine the Brutus/Portia scene more closely to highlight some of them.

ANALYSIS

As you know by now, I believe that storytelling is the primary function of the actor—to get across to the audience the story the playwright has written. It follows that an actor must begin her work by understanding what the story is.

Everyone recognizes a story when they hear one, but this recognition is a passive kind, and when called upon to recount the story we have just been told, we realize it may be a little bit more complicated than it seems. What things are important to the story and can't be excluded? What things are details that are not essential? How do character, action, and dialogue relate? And most importantly, what are the stepping-stone moments in a story that must be clearly rendered if the story is going to work for an audience? All these questions, yet I haven't even mentioned conflict, the engine of drama, or objective-playing, the primary acting tool that that springs from that conflict.

Actors need practice at recognizing the story they will have to tell, and you won't get enough practice by working on one or two scenes a year. Why not spend some time developing the skill? Why not assemble a series of short scenes for yourself and read each one? After reading the play, try writing a paragraph recounting the story in your own words. The narrative you write should focus on action, not description. It should include all the cause-and-effect actions of the story. By learning how to do this well, you will develop the ability to see the work you must deliver in terms of a series of actions. You'll probably also discover where the moments are that you should be playing clearly and effectively. And you will get a sense that actions are as important as the words, if not more so. This kind of process was introduced to you at the beginning of this book, but if you're serious about mining a script effectively on your own, it's time that you put in the time to truly develop your skills.

Read the story summaries you produce for their completeness, effectiveness, and accuracy. It will probably be amazing how much you leave out at first, and how much your written interpretation might differ from the play when you go back to it. Your job will be figure out whether what you have written is accurate and effective, and where you took liberties or omitted things that would negatively affect the telling of the good and accurate story.

The scene from *Julius Caesar* that my two students were working on is short, yet it has a great dramatic arc with plenty of conflict. Here is how a cause-and-effect summary of the scene might look:

Portia finds Brutus outside in the orchard at their home after noticing that he is not in bed. She had gotten up to search for him. Brutus is surprised to see his wife and is concerned that she will catch cold in the damp early morning. Portia expresses her equal concern for his health. She then goes on to describe a series of strange behaviors that Brutus has exhibited, as though something very pressing has been churning up his mind. The description includes short-temperedness, impatience, sighing, and rudeness. Portia confesses to having held her tongue, but Brutus's leaving of the bed so early in the morning forces her to ask him to tell her what is wrong. Brutus tries to pass off his behavior as a result of not feeling well. But Portia will not have it. She counters that Brutus is too smart to walk around in the cold and damp, and if he were sick, he would do something about it. Brutus tries to get her to go back to bed. She ignores him and continues to make the case that Brutus would not do stupid, damaging things to his health. No, she tells him, something else is bothering him, something that is sickening his mind. She begs him to share his concerns with her by literally getting down on her knees before him. She begs to know who the men were that he had been talking to, and more importantly what they wanted. Brutus affectionately pleads with her to get off her knees. As Portia does so, she asks her husband to treat her with the love and respect that she deserves—by sharing with her the details of his troubles. Otherwise, she will draw the conclusion that she is good enough for the bed and domestic responsibility, but not good enough to be his equal partner. Brutus counters that she is his love and his equal. Portia counters back that if she were, her husband would share all with her. She reminds him that she can be trusted, pointing to the scar where she once stabbed herself in the leg to prove her loyalty and devotion. Brutus is moved and gives in to his wife. As he is about to share his troubles, there is a knocking at the door. Brutus promises to tell his wife all later, even as he whisks her from the room.

That is a fairly detailed cause-and-effect rendering. Yet even so, actable details are probably left out. But if you were to read this narrative without having read Shakespeare's text, you would still have a pretty good fix on how to play the scene from the map the paragraph provides. In addition, the process of writing the cause-and-effect sequence makes it easy to identify the conflict contained in the scene and the individual objectives that each of the characters plays. The relationship based on mutual love and respect, which my own actors missed so completely in their first read, is also readily apparent. The significant moments are clear. It's easy to find the physical actions suggested in the script, and the reasons for them are more obvious. Finally, significant words that might have been glossed over in a general reading now stand out sharply, making themselves clear in terms of how to use them in the scene. If you develop the ability to do this kind of work and truly commit to using it, you will be far less likely to bring in a scene that seems flat and goes nowhere.

The exercise of translating a scene into a prose narrative forces you to see the scene in terms of action, not dialogue. This is essential if you are to get out of the habit of treating a script as a repository of words to be said and nothing more. You must develop the habit of thinking of a script as a combination of dialogue and actions, implied or stated clearly—a pairing in which neither is more important than the other in the quest of good storytelling.

SYNTHESIS — FINDING THE ACTION

Once you have a fairly specific and detailed picture of the action of the scene, you might want to think about it in terms of the cause-and-effect sequence of events that unfolds through both the dialogue and what the characters do. If you focus only on dialogue, you may get caught up in the task of delivering the dialogue accurately at the expense of telling the story clearly through actions and by making moments. Getting the words right will be important later, but at this point you want to concentrate on action.

You might want to ask yourself a leading question like, "What are some *as ifs* you can use for your scene?" An *as if* is a situation from your real life that might be analogous to the one you are playing. You could ask yourself, for instance, if you have ever had a boyfriend who was obviously troubled and didn't want to talk about it. Did you manage to get him to talk? How did you do it? The tactics you used, if you were successful, were probably not unlike those that Portia uses in the scene.

Shakespeare, of course, supplies the dialogue in the Portia/Brutus scene, but he does not tell the actors what mustard and relish to put on the words to make them believable and effective. Delivering the lines without the necessary condiments, as my actors did, will fail to produce believable work. It will also cause you to focus on your own lines rather than on your partner's reactions to what you do and the manner in which he does it. What I am talking about here are tactics. The dialogue must be put across in a certain way in order for it to be effective. The audience must see why and how Brutus relents. It is ultimately up to the actors to make that happen believably, moment to moment, in a clear and interesting sequence.

The actor playing Brutus will be helped by an *as if,* too. If you are playing Brutus, you might ask yourself if you have ever been pressured into confessing to someone you love something you would rather keep to yourself. What is that pressure like? How does it make you feel? How, in turn, does it make you behave physically? What do you say to avoid giving up the information you're trying to conceal? Is there eye contact? Is it maintained? When might it be broken? What tactics did you use to get your loving interrogator out of the room? What things did you do physically to make that happen? If, as Brutus, you can come up with a range of ideas for movement, you will probably be able to move believably and effectively. If you can stay close to the ideas of the dialogue and are able to move through the cause-and-effect sequence of actions, you will find many usable things that can be transferred into the actual scene when you rehearse it.

I had my Brutus and Portia improv their scene once we had clearly established the cause-and-effect arc of the story. Their improv was far better than their reading in terms of moments, clarity of progression, their relationship, all the basics. They listened to each other, and by doing so they found physical things to do—movement, gesture, and business. They connected need with moving closer, and they showed love by the way they touched each other and by the way they made or avoided eye contact. The physical contact, in turn, caused reactions that were physical, and these reactions began to delineate moments.

Since it was an improv, my actors listened to each other far better than they had when they were reading. They had to generate their own dialogue in response to what the partner was saying, so they listened to each other intently. And those things were said for defined and specific reasons, and what was said landed, again causing a reaction. Of course, the dialogue was not quite as poetic as Shakespeare's, but what was lost in poetry was more than made up for in terms of clarity of action and dramatic progression.

By the time we were finished playing with the improv, my actors had plenty to work with for their next rehearsal outside of class. Before I let them go, however, I had them reread their scene using the actual dialogue. All of it was clearer. The dramatic progression emerged, the ingredients of a believable husband-and-wife relationship were there, and the physical actions that real people might take on were already starting to develop.

LISTENING

Listening onstage is not just about listening. It refers to using all the senses. When we listen in life we listen to the words and try to determine what they mean—literally, contextually, and subtextually. We also use clues like body language to help us decipher what is communicated. We are sensitive to the nuances we see as well as hear. We respond to the give-and-take of touch and eye contact and physical proximity. We often use those powers to great effect without thinking about them. But an actor must be available to see and hear and feel those things when they happen, because they will breathe life into her work.

It is also true that in life we can often learn far more from the manner in which something is said than from the words themselves. Chekhov used this understanding about the way we communicate to bring forth a whole new kind of playwriting. In his major plays, what the characters say is often far less important than what they do while they're talking. This aspect of human communication must become a part of any actor's work. If an actor's eyes and focus are on the script, she will never find the tango steps she is supposed to be dancing moment by moment with her scene partner. The actors who get professional work are constantly connected with each other on the stage. They see and hear and feel what the audience sees. They are no less aware of nuance onstage than they would be in life. Perhaps they are more so.

You must force yourself to listen with all your senses. You must look at your partner rather than at the page, even when you're just reading a scene. Look down at your script only to get the next sentence; then look up, and deliver it directly into the eyes of your scene partner. Make him react before allowing him to return to the script to find his next piece of dialogue. When you're listening, be sure that you're looking at your scene partner while she speaks. Keep in mind that in this stage of rehearsal, the accuracy of the line is not as important as playing the action suggested by the line. An audience will forgive a wrong word, but a lost moment is far harder to make up for.

Every moment is a brick on the road to the Emerald City. Get off the road, and you're lost.

When actors truly listen, they see and hear and feel the moments. They sense the progression of the scene, even if their analysis is a bit off the mark. You must break the habit of reading a scene disconnected from the partner you are dancing with. Really listening to a scene partner makes an actor find moments. Too many young actors don't do this. Instead of listening, they simply wait for the cue to say the next line. When they hear the cue line, or when they hear the pause, signaling the end of the partner's speech, they recite their line, either without purpose or in a generalized fashion. Even as the words come out their mouths, their minds are on the next set of lines they have to say. If this is what you are doing, you cannot be playing the action of the line, you cannot be in the moment.

Now for an easy exercise you can do with your scene partner before putting up a scene for your class. It will improve your listening and your commitment to playing the action of a line. If you are still on book, be sure that you look down at your script, take in a line or two, and then look up at your partner before saying the line. The line must be completely delivered to your partner. You may not go on until you can do this. Neither you nor your partner can go back to the script until the line has been delivered and until the listening partner has taken it in. If you fail to do this, you must repeat the delivery and receipt of the line. This will be difficult at first, but if you and your partner hold to it, you will very quickly sense a change toward a more believable delivery of the line and a better connection between what is said and how the next line is delivered.

Once you are able to do this, you are ready for the next exercise. Here it is. After your partner says her first line, you will simply say, "What?" as though you hadn't heard the line or didn't quite understand it. Your partner will then repeat the line with significantly more intensity. When you are satisfied with the intensity, you may say your line. Your partner will then offer up her "What?" until she is satisfied with your intensity.

It would go something like this:

PORTIA: Brutus, my lord.
YOU: *What?!*
PORTIA: Brutus, my lord.

You: *What?!*
PORTIA: Brutus, my lord.
BRUTUS: Portia, what mean you?
You: *What?!*
BRUTUS: Portia, what mean you?
BRUTUS: Wherefore rise you now?

Each time the line is repeated, in all probability it will be stronger, more specific, and more directed to produce a result in your scene partner. Usually, by the second or third time the actor says the line, it has begun to sound like good, compelling acting. In fact, you'll probably discover that if you said all your lines that way the first time, you would have one heck of a scene. So take what you've learned from the exercises and put it into your scene.

If lack of listening is an issue that rings a bell for you, consider reading some books by Sanford Meisner. Meisner's lifetime work focused heavily on getting actors to listen in the moment, and he created many exciting exercises that might work for you. You could explore the possibility of studying with an acting teacher who is proficient in Meisner technique, as well.

Before I close this chapter, you might be interested to know that when my Brutus and Portia put up their scene again, it was light-years better. In fact, it was excellent. Their relationship was clear, the arc of the scene was apparent, the stakes were high. Their movement and gestures seemed natural, yet clearly helped define the moments and the progression in the scene. All of the moments were there, defined and very full. In short, these were actors I'd consider for work. I was proud and happy. They were capable of doing this on their own the first time. So why didn't they? That is an issue I continue to explore in my teaching work, and when I come up with a stronger theory on why students try so hard to avoid the craft that will help them, I'll be sure to share it with you.

In the meantime, there is a lot here for you to consider. Ultimately, you will need to learn how to travel alone. In the pages of this book you have been offered a map that will lead you to the veins of gold you will need for building a reliable craft. It is now up to you to learn to mine your script effectively. The gold is there waiting for you.

CHAPTER TWELVE

PROCESSING THE GOLD—A REVIEW

DURING THE COURSE OF THIS BOOK, YOU HAVE SPENT A lot of time learning how to examine a script and find the story it contains. You have worked on your ability to find the story and make choices that will best serve it and the character you play. So after all this analysis work, I wonder if you can define one. I mean, what exactly is a story?

This might be more difficult than you first thought, right?

We are exposed to stories almost from the moment we are born, and they become a central part of our lives, right up to the time we die. Yet most of us take stories for granted, in the same way we accept that a cell phone rings or that our computers tell us just about everything we need to know. We recognize stories when we hear them and even make snap judgments about which ones are good or bad. But most of us can't really define what stories are, what makes them effective or not, and, most importantly, how they work. But as theater people, we need to know all about stories. They are the lifeblood of our existence. After all, as you hopefully are now well aware, as actors you are first and foremost storytellers.

By now you have come to realize that it is a playwright's job to come up with a good story and tell it well through a combination of dialogue and stage direction. Playwrights have to master the mechanics of their craft if they are to dependably build their stories into good ones. But, as an actor, it is your job to recognize the mechanics the playwright has given you and make the work come to life through the choices you make based on what you read in the script. Yet the playwright never speaks directly to you, telling you what to do.

It is up to you, then, to be able to take what the playwright has given you and make the story come to life — through your imagination, yes, but first by understanding the story you are given and then by making it work. This requires that you understand what a story is and how to tell it as well or better than the playwright did. The difference is that the playwright creates from scratch, but actors engage in an interpretive art. You must examine the "music" the playwright scores for you by analyzing it before you can play it effectively. Only once you understand it through analysis, inference, and deduction can you hope to play the playwright's music effectively and add to it with your own special artistry.

Since we're almost at the end of our journey together, take a moment now and ask yourself if when you read your next script, you will stop to ask yourself the question, "What is the story I'm reading here, anyway?" In spite of the fact that in this book we have been talking about story at all times, it will take discipline and commitment on your part to get into the habit of asking yourself the questions that must be asked. But this is exactly what you will have to do — if you really want to become an effective actor/storyteller.

The American Heritage Dictionary defines *story* as "an account or recital of an event or a series of events, either true or fictitious." It defines *event* as "a. something that takes place; an occurrence" or "b. a *significant* occurrence or happening." If you're like many beginning actors, you probably used to start your exploration of a script thinking in terms of character and emotion. But remember, the definition of *story* focuses on events, *things that happen — significant occurrences*. Events make for stories, and significant events make for good stories. Thinking in terms of character and emotion doesn't necessarily plug you in to the machinery of story-making. You have learned in these pages that you will serve yourself better as an actor to think initially in terms of the events that make up a story, and about your part in the creation and execution of those events.

Before we finish, try the following exercise. It might help you reset the way you ultimately approach the acting process, if you are still struggling with the concept of actor as storyteller.

Look at these two sentences:

The boy was sad.
The boy tripped and fell.

Which is more interesting? Which comes closer to the idea of a story as defined earlier?

Now read these two sentences together:

The boy tripped and fell.
The boy cried.

Compare your reaction to this pair of sentences to the first pair. You probably liked the way the second pair worked together more than the first one. Why? Probably because the second pair of sentences is much closer to a story. There is a sequence of events with a beginning, middle, and end. "The boy cried" might be described as an event. "The boy was sad" — not as event-like.

Now think for a minute. In terms of story, what essential element is still missing from our better pair of sentences? Of course you could tell me character development, or time and place specifics — the given circumstances of the situation — and you wouldn't be wrong. Any story profits from a set of clearly defined specifics, but we're talking right now about essentials — of building a story through the things that happen. If you've been paying attention during the course of this book, you know that I'm talking about the C word of drama — *conflict*, often known as the engine of drama. We know that conflict occurs when something comes between someone and his purpose, objective, mission, or need. See what happens to the story when some conflict is added in.

The boy was running fast.
He saw a snake in front of him.
He swerved to avoid it.
The boy tripped and fell.
The boy cried.

Now the story seems to have a beginning, middle, and end, as well as a conflict and an *arc*. The arc is the journey the actor as character goes through during a story—generally, the bigger the arc, the more interesting the story. So with all these "good story" boxes now checked, is the story the best it's going to be in terms of dramatic events? Is there anything further we can improve storywise while just sticking with simple essentials? I'll give you a hint. Take another look at the conflict. Read on when you've done some thinking on how to improve what we've got so far—by playing with the conflict.

Since conflict is the engine of drama, it stands to reason that the more the conflict is maximized, the better the story will be. By the same token, the bigger and better the story arc, the better the story will be.

The boy was running fast.
He saw a snake in front of him.
He swerved to avoid it.
He fought to keep his balance.
The boy tripped and fell.
The boy cried.

Better, right? The boy's fight to keep his balance kept the conflict going longer, and it added a bit of suspense before reaching the outcome. This is what good storytellers want to do, and since actors are storytellers, it is your job as an actor to maximize what the playwright has given you. Though in his stage directions the playwright might not have told you to fight to keep your balance, the good actor will add his own storytelling details—details that will enhance the story without changing its direction. Starting your examination of a script by thinking in these terms is a great way to begin fulfilling your storytelling responsibilities to that script. This is the gold you've been looking for.

Keep in mind that the manner in which you physically carry out these preliminary choices later in the process can and will suggest character. For example, will the boy cry with abandon, or will he fight to keep from crying? These are choices. What does each say about the character? Which choice would be better for the story? Why? There is never a single right answer, by the way. There are good choices and better choices. Good choices serve and enhance the story being told. There *are* bad choices, however. Bad choices are those that go against the story or that somehow contradict the story's logic or move away from its essential railroad tracks provided by the playwright.

Of course, there are still more things you can do with the basics offered in the six-line version of our story. Take the arc, for instance. If, for example, running makes the boy happy and running fast is his idea of paradise, then the arc from bliss to crying is a bigger one than the six lines seem to provide. That interpretation will improve the arc and the story. Or if, when the boy falls, he falls close to or into the snake, the conflict elements will be heightened. Again, the story is enhanced. You get the idea. All of the suggestions in this little exercise stem from the idea of thinking as a storyteller, and they are all ideas that work to improve the story. If you don't start to think in these terms, then what you choose to do will, at least in terms of the story, be accidental. Working from craft rather than luck will make your work far more successful—consistently. And that is what craft is for. And that is where the gold can be found.

In this exercise the focus was on events or actions, but playwrights obviously rely far more heavily on dialogue, which may suggest the events that are unfolding, but do not necessarily spell those events out. When reading a script, actors must learn to decipher the dialogue in such a way that they can see through to the storytelling events that occur. Characters are not always direct about what they think and feel, and playwrights don't necessarily point the actors in the right direction. They assume that actors will hold up their end of the dramatic bargain by finding and executing the story contained within the script. Once you can do this, that, too, is gold.

All right. So here's another exercise, but this time instead of a list of events, you will find some actual dialogue from a play. It will take more work to find the events that make up a story here, since the events are masked within the dialogue. See if you can piece together what is going on. In this play, the given circumstances (purposely not provided here) are very important to the story. But don't worry about that for the moment. Just work from the premise that your job as an actor is to tell the story. Using only what's given, see what you can come up with. You might want to jot down all the clues you can find and briefly write a note for each as to what you think the clues suggest. Doing that will help you when you try to put all the clues together to make a story out of this excerpt.

[NICKI *enters. She is wearing a pink dress and a green belt. She runs to a mirror and examines herself. As she does so, she hears laughter from the next room.*]

NICKI: Oh crap! I'm so late. They're already sitting down. At least my hair doesn't look too bad.

[OLIVIA *enters from within.*]

OLIVIA: Finally. We were so worried about you. [*Kisses her.*] Are you all right?
NICKI: I'm fine. Just a little nervous. You have so-o-o much company. Happy birthday, sweetie.
OLIVIA: Don't you worry about anything. Everyone here is a friend. Oh, honey. Pink and green. I'm not so sure about that.
NICKI: Really? The belt isn't really green though. It's more neutral than green, isn't it?

[OLIVIA *takes* NICKI*'s hands and leads her into the reception room.*]

Before taking one last look at the analysis process we have been working on in this book, it is probably worth mentioning one final time that we should always start with the story or possible stories that a script is telling. Remember, the good playwright includes only what is essential. As an actor, you must assume that everything you find in a script is there for a reason. With that in mind, even the most offhand remark or gesture suddenly takes on importance as you begin your detective work. So what did you write down as your clues? Here's my list.

Nicki is late. It's Olivia's birthday party.

Pink and green—don't go together.

Nicki examines herself in mirror and comments on her hair—concern with how she looks.

Lots of guests.

She's nervous about the party.

Olivia says she was worried. Tries to reassure Nicki about the other guests. Comments negatively about Nicki's color combination.

They call each other "honey" and "sweetie."

Nicki tries to justify her color choice.

Olivia pulls Nicki into the party without resolving the color issue.

Does your list look something like mine? Maybe you saw something I missed. If so, address it in the next step. Now you're a detective, Sherlock, or CSI officer; it's your job to put the clues together and come up with a story to play. On the assumption that everything is important, write a scenario of the story based on your evidence. Read on after you have written your report, Detective.

Here's a scenario based on my collected clues.

Nicki enters on the run. She is late for Olivia's birthday party. She stops and listens to the noise and laughter from the next room. She then rushes to the mirror. She checks herself closely. She plays with her hair and smiles. Olivia enters and kisses Nicki warmly. She then makes Nicki uncomfortable when she inadvertently comments on Nicki's color combination. They like each other a lot, however, because they call each other terms of endearment. Olivia pulls Nicki into the party without patching up the color-clash issue.

How does your scenario compare to mine? Notice that mine uses the clues I had assembled and essentially reports in terms of event moments. I also made a few inferences and deductions based on the clues assembled. These refer to thoughts, feelings, and motivations regarding the characters — things I can't really know but that either the dialogue or actions suggest. Since these inferences are not facts, they may be contradicted if and when more information becomes available.

For the most part, I have accepted all of the dialogue at face value. In other words, I have interpreted the dialogue based on its *literal meaning*. There are no given circumstances available to tell me otherwise. So when Olivia calls Nicki "honey," I accept the literal meaning. She is being affectionate. As story detectives, we should accept that characters are telling the truth unless we have reason to not believe them. If we did not follow this protocol as actors, it would make dialogue impossible to handle — too many possibilities. In life, we generally accept what others tell us as true unless we have reason to think otherwise, or unless the circumstances suggest that we are not necessarily being told the truth. The way we hear and use dialogue onstage, just as in life, must be influenced by what we know about people and about the situations at hand. As a result, what we say and hear is often colored by *context* and *subtext*.

Keep in mind that dialogue often has *contextual* and *subtextual* meaning as well as a literal meaning. This contextual and subtextual meaning is often far more important than the literal kind. *Contextual meaning* refers to how what we say is influenced by the circumstances under which we say it. An "I love you" may mean something far different when said to a lover in private than it does when said to a friend in a social context. But many things we say have a subtextual meaning, as well. *Subtextual meaning* refers to dialogue that may hide a much deeper meaning or be used as a filler for thoughts and feelings that the speaker does not wish to reveal.

In a Chekhov play, characters seldom express their true thoughts and feelings about each other, yet the actor must know what those thoughts and feelings are so that they can shape the story in spite of the fact that the dialogue does not help them do so, at least not directly. For these kinds of reasons, in our preparation for doing a play, we must read the script many times, just as a detective goes over a crime scene again and again looking for new clues and trying to put them together coherently. With repeated readings, we learn more and more about the story and how events, actions, and characters interrelate. As a result, we begin to see more deeply into what is really being said and done, as well as what is not. In turn, we learn how to best shape the unfolding story.

One last note before we move on. You may have noticed that my scenario was not the most exciting story ever told. For one thing, it lacked conflict, and for another, its arc was not exactly major. Perhaps this section of a bigger story was more expositional than climactic, and perhaps the material itself does not allow for a large arc. That does not, however, release you as an actor from looking for potential story-making elements. Your job is to make the story as compelling and clear as the script allows.

So with all this in mind, let's go back to the scene. But before we do, let me add some given circumstances that I did not reveal before. These added ingredients may increase the potential for conflict and improve the flattish arc that we currently have. Okay, here goes. Suppose that Olivia is the oldest sibling in a well-to-do family. Suppose that her brother, Andrew, is dating Nicki, a girl from the poor side of town. No one in Olivia's family likes Nicki, except, of course, for her brother. This is the first time that Nicki has been invited to a family function.

Take a close look at the dialogue again. Given what you now know about context and subtext, could you make any changes in the scenario that would strengthen it in terms of story? Think about how you might play the dialogue now that you have this added information. Think about all this before reading on.

Here I will repeat the scene, but I have added some acting comments based on the given circumstances that are now a part of the story. Given what I now know, I will consider the dialogue and action more in terms of their possible contextual and subtextual meaning.

> [NICKI *enters. She is wearing a pink dress and a green belt. She runs to a mirror and examines herself.* **[She's nervous and self-conscious because she's meeting a bunch of people who may be above her, and also, they're probably very judgmental. She is insecure.]** *As she does so, she hears laughter from the next room.*]

NICKI: Oh crap! I'm so late. They're already sitting down. At least my hair doesn't look too bad. **[It's her hair that she thinks looks good. What about the rest of her?]**

[OLIVIA *enters from within.*]

OLIVIA: Finally. **[Does this mean, "It's about time, you moron"?]** We were worried about you. **[Is this sincere?]** [*Kisses her.*] **[Is the kiss sincere? How does she do it?]** Are you all right?

NICKI: I'm fine. Just a little nervous. You have so much company. Happy birthday, sweetie. **[Is the word "sweetie" sincere?]**

OLIVIA: Don't you worry about anything. Everyone here is a friend. Oh, honey. **[Is she discovering the colors only now? Is she doing this to undermine Nicki's confidence?]** Pink and green. I'm not so sure about that.

NICKI: Really? The belt isn't really green though. It's more neutral than green, isn't it?

[**Is she trying to retain some dignity, or does she really think so?**] [OLIVIA *takes* NICKI's *hands and leads her into the reception room.*] [**Is Olivia ignoring Nicki here to get Nicki past a difficult moment, or is she dragging Nicki in to meet the hostile crowd while Nicki is still recovering?**]

Look at all the questions that are raised when you consider the dialogue in terms of context and subtext. It certainly increases the range of story possibilities, doesn't it? So how do you know which are the right answers to the questions raised? The short answer is you don't. But that is why reading for the story is so important. At least when you decide what the story you are telling is, it helps narrow down the range of choices; and keep in mind that your mandate is to tell the best story you can while staying on the tracks provided by the playwright— that will serve as your compass through the script.

Once you determine what the story is, you can begin to narrow down the choices you must make as the character you have been cast in. Suppose, for instance, that you have been cast as Olivia. You must determine—on the simplest level—whether she is a "good guy" or a "bad guy." Of course, a good character-centered realistic play will give us characters who have both good qualities and some not-so-good ones, but again, we are just beginning our exploration. It is always worth asking whether or not the audience is supposed to root for the character we are playing. For the purpose of making a point, let me give you some more information. In this play, we come to find out that Olivia's family is wonderful, and that Nicki only pretends to love Andrew in order to marry him and improve her station in life. By the end of the play, through her conniving, Nicki actually runs the family, and we, as the audience, are supposed to hate her.

So with this information in hand, if you are the actor playing Olivia, will you now play her as sweetly as you can because she's a good guy? And if you're playing Nicki, will you play her as though you have a black hat and moustache? The answer is no, of course not. This is a realistic play in which the characters should come off as real people. That means that they, like all human beings, are a mosaic of characteristics. Which characteristics will you play? That's a trick question, really. In fact, you will need to play your objectives, which come from the conflict. But again, what you want and need must emerge from what the story requires.

Now we're ready for the next step — objectives. Objectives arise from the conflict, but the cutting from this play contains only a hint of conflict since, in truth, this scene comes very early in the play. But because you now know what happens later in the play, you can infer that Nicki wants to ingratiate herself to the family. She can't take it over until she is a part of it. So let's say that Nicki wants to win over Olivia — the first member of the family she runs into. And since we now know that Olivia is kind, and doesn't yet know what Nicki has up her sleeve, she wants to make Nicki comfortable.

Let's take one last look at the scene, with the characters' objectives in mind, and see how that new knowledge affects our take on the dialogue on all three of its levels.

> Nicki's objective — to make the family and therefore Olivia like her.
> Olivia's objective — to make Nicki feel at ease.

> [NICKI *enters. She is wearing a pink dress and a green belt. She runs to a mirror and examines herself.* **[To examine herself — if she looks good, it will help make a good impression.]** *As she does so, she hears laughter from the next room.*] **[Obstacle to her objective — all those people to win over.]**

NICKI: Oh crap! I'm so late. They're already sitting down. At least my hair doesn't look too bad. **[Encourages herself that she can play her objective and win it.]**

> [OLIVIA *enters from within.*]

OLIVIA: Finally. **[To show Nicki that she has been worried and concerned; to make Nicki feel that she is worthy of Olivia's concern. Or an expression of her subtext that leaked out and must now be covered?]** We were worried about you. [*Kisses her.*] Are you all right? **[To make Nicki feel wanted and at ease — a verbal tactic to fulfill her objective.]**

NICKI: I'm fine. Just a little nervous. **[To show her honesty — a tactic for her objective.]** You have so much company. **[Suggests**

insecurity and will play to Olivia's need to make people comfy.] Happy birthday, sweetie. **[Direct pursuit of her objective.]**

OLIVIA: Don't you worry about anything. Everyone here is a friend. **[Direct playing of objective.]** Oh, honey. Pink and green. I'm not so sure about that. **[A discovery of an obstacle that will stand in the way of Nicki being accepted and therefore being comfortable. Then an attempt to cover the judgment.]**

NICKI: Really? The belt isn't really green though. It's more neutral than green, isn't it? **[Tactic to get around fashion faux pas.]**

[OLIVIA *takes* NICKI's *hands and leads her into the reception room.*] **[Tactic to show support, or getting past the obstacle of the moment?]**

In terms of playing objectives in this version of the scene, I have made very direct choices for each of the characters based on the stated objectives. Olivia is good and sticks to her objective of making Nicki feel comfortable at all times. Nicki sticks with tactics that might ingratiate herself with Olivia. But these are not the only choices possible. Other objectives may be at play here, and these may lead to more complexity of character and more interesting scene dynamics. Suffice it to say that with slightly different objectives, the lines of dialogue might lend themselves to a much larger palette of subtextual and contextual meaning than this particular interpretation generates.

Suppose, for example, Olivia's objective is to scare Nicki off. If so, she might say "Pink and green" in a horrified manner without masking it. If her objective is to scare Nicki away without letting her know it, she might say it in a horrified tone and then try to mask it with sweetness in the next line. That would be a well-played tactic. As you can imagine, with some interpretations, subtext and context might come heavily into play. Some choices, of course, will depend on how your acting partner chooses to deliver her lines as a result of her objective playing. Obviously, if unkindness is heard, it will affect the way Nicki reacts, overtly or covertly. But analyzing a scene for its potential is always the best way of entering a rehearsal process. Preparation choices can and should be changed as needed.

In reality, the Nicki/Olivia scene is my own adaptation of a short scene that occurs early in Anton Chekhov's *Three Sisters*. In the play, Olga, the oldest of the three sisters, is a kind and selfless person. But she is also interested in making sure her family is protected. Natasha, who later gets control of the family through her marriage to Olga's brother, Andre, is first and foremost a selfish social climber. How the actor playing Olga can both be kind and protect her family interests becomes an interesting challenge for the actor playing her. The actor who plays Natasha has the equally difficult challenge of making a potentially one-dimensional monster seem as complex, believable, and human as possible. The most effective way of accomplishing these goals is by finding tactics and objectives that are interesting and multicolored yet serve the overall needs of the story. Failing to pay significant primary attention to the story and its arc in the early goings will make this challenge difficult, if not impossible. Seeing dialogue and action through the prism of context and subtext is an essential skill that all actors must be able to master — if you are to become a master storyteller.

ASSAYING
THE GOLD

CRAFT BY DEFINITION IS A SKILL THAT CAN BE LEARNED.
Unlike talent, which is God-given or genetic, or art, which is far more nebulous, craft is something that with practice you can master—to varying degrees, of course, depending on your dedication and commitment. The set of skills that make up a craft can be learned—mostly by doing. That means that every student of craft is capable of learning to do it. Craft is what you should focus on.

Acting craft, like all craft, has a set of tools that can be learned. And like all craft, mastery begins with the basics. Once mastered, you can build on that foundation. Understanding a script and how it works is essential to your basic craft. And it is more about practicing the mechanics than anything else. Common sense and a defined process are what you need.

Here again is a summary of the process that has been defined in the pages of this book:

Analysis—taking the play apart effectively

Determining the overall story of the play

 The central conflict and all other conflicts found in the play

 The cause-and-effect sequence of the story overall and scene by scene

What the story is trying to tell us — its thematic elements

How the character relates to the overall story and the central conflict of the play; the character's specific conflicts

The character's purpose in the story

The character's objectives overall and scene by scene, related to the characters sharing the stage with that character

The risks, stakes, and obstacles that the character faces

The character's arc (his journey of change through the play)

The character's big moments

Synthesis — putting together what you will do onstage

Finding and executing a body of actions — physical and psychological, for each moment of the play — that leads to what the character needs while serving the story

Listening and reacting

Getting all the previous stuff into your body so that you are free to listen and react to the moments spontaneously yet purposefully as those moments unfold onstage

Remember, you must be able to read your map and understand it. That's what a script is, and that is what is required of you. At the other end of this process, the vein of gold awaits you. This vein will make you rich. You will find all the gold you will ever need as an actor in the pages of your script. Accept this fact and work toward mastery. Demand of yourself that you learn to read well. Learn to effectively analyze for plot and character, and for where the story events are. Learn to see how a plot progresses in each script you take on. Don't forget that actors *are* storytellers. You must understand the story before you can do your part in the telling of it.

If you keep at it, I promise you that before long, you will be able to find the gold in every script that comes your way. And that is worth working for!

ACKNOWLEDGMENTS

I would like to thank the team at Hal Leonard—especially John Cerullo, Marybeth Keating, and Angela Hardin; John for his confidence in me, Marybeth for keeping the train on time and running smoothly, and Angela for making everything better. Also to all my dear friends and colleagues who took a look and made the book cleaner, clearer, and more useful. Thank you all.

GLOSSARY OF ACTING TERMS

ACTING

The most common definition I have seen goes something like this: "behaving believably under fictional circumstances." And that certainly describes the process. However, a more useful definition—one that I have come to employ over the years—might be the one that defines *good* acting. It goes something like this: "acting that is believable and that tells the best possible story while serving the script." All actors, of course, must be believable. The audience must accept an actor's work as she moves through the world of the play in a step-by-step sequence of action. *Believable* is not synonymous with *realistic,* however. A nonrealistic play may require choices that are not necessarily realistic but are consistent with the universe created by the playwright. The actor wants to tell the best possible story, as well—one that is the most interesting she can possibly create. That story, however, must be consistent with the intentions of the playwright and the production. Hugely entertaining choices by a character that are inconsistent with the overall needs of the play or production cannot be considered good acting choices. Each actor must make choices that contribute to the whole of the play and, like pieces of a jigsaw puzzle, fit perfectly with the pieces that surround her character.

ACTION

This term has several meanings pertinent to the acting process. *Action* can refer to the cause-and-effect sequence of events in a play—essential for understanding the given plot and for making choices that are consistent with and supportive of that plot. This kind of action can also be referred to as the *throughline* or *arc.* The term *action* can also apply to any physical or psychological activity an actor carries out in the course of the play, as in,

"What is the action you are playing?" This kind of action is more frequently called an actor's *objective* or *intention*. Keep in mind that no matter which definition of action is employed, action is an essential ingredient of drama and closely relates to the engine of all drama — conflict. Actors who focus on emotion or character, rather than action, are in danger of falling into theatrical quicksand, for — as Stanislavski came to believe — actions are doable, whereas playing emotion or character directly is less so.

ADLER, STELLA

A member of one of the most famous acting families in America and one of the original members of the Group Theatre who challenged Lee Strasberg's interpretations of Stanislavski's system. She later went to Paris and studied with the Russian master herself. Upon her return, she explained to the Group Theatre Stanislavski's most recent theories of acting, which focused on physical action. Lee Strasberg rejected these ideas and began referring to Stanislavski's earlier emotional work as "the Method," the technique he later became universally famous for. Adler, too, went on to become one of America's foremost acting teachers, focusing on physical and psychological action, imagination, and the use of the script.

ANALYSIS AND SYNTHESIS

The intellectual tools necessary for breaking down a script and putting it back together so that it will work effectively for an audience. Good acting begins with an understanding of the play and the ability to make acting choices that serve that understanding. Contrary to the beliefs of some, acting is not simply about actors being able to personalize their feeling onto a script, but rather about communicating what characters think and feel to an audience so that the audience will understand the story of the play as written by the playwright — the story crafted by the combined choices of actors and directors to be as compelling and clear as possible.

ARC

Also known as the *action* or *throughline,* the *arc* refers the journey each character makes through the course of a scene or play, or to the sequential action of the play overall. It is essential that actors recognize and respond to each of the sequential events of the play and make choices as the character that demonstrate how these events affect and alter them. The bigger the arc, the greater the journey, and the more the character changes during the course of the play. In general, the bigger the difference between the character at the end of the play and at the beginning, the more interesting the performance, and the more interesting the play—provided the audience sees the actor making those changes as the character. It is up to the actors to understand the journey made by their characters and to communicate it through their chosen actions.

AS IF

An acting tool in which an actor finds an analogous situation from his life in order to find a way to play a script's specific given circumstances. Recalling what it was like when you broke up with your girlfriend, for instance, might help you understand the given circumstances between Jim and Laura in that famous scene from.

BEAT

The length of script during which an actor plays a particular objective, tactic, or action. A beat is always preceded by a transition and followed by another. The term, coined by Stanislavski, is actually the result of a pronunciation of the word *bit* with a Russian accent, although there is a logic to the word *beat,* as well. A particular beat (recognizable pattern or rhythm) is played until a victory, defeat, or discovery, or new information, causes the beat to end. When this occurs, a transition occurs, at which point a new beat is established and played. As Stanislavski probably originally meant it, one bit (or small section of action) is followed by another and another, creating the throughline of the scene.

BEGINNINGS, MIDDLES, AND ENDS

The necessary steps that an actor must go through for all effective storytelling. Plays, scenes, beats, and even moments have beginnings, middles, and ends. So do all physical actions. Actors who fail to find the beginnings, middles, and ends to actions, moments, or any other aspects of their work will fail to be believable and will fail to execute choices that are clear and compelling for an audience. Most actions, for instance, start with the reason for the action. The actor who ignores this fact jumps into a middle and fails to communicate believably the story sequence he is undertaking. Dialogue, for instance, doesn't begin with the first word. It begins with the need to speak. Beginning actors doing a monologue often begin with the words rather than the need to speak. Because of this, it often takes them several moments before they connect with the words they are saying. The words have been wasted, and the actor looks bad. Here is another example. Try yawning. If you started with opening your mouth, you probably failed to execute a believable yawn. Yawns start with the impulse to yawn. So does an acting moment. The yawn is complete, not when the physical action of yawning is complete, but when the result that the yawn produces in the yawner is apparent to the yawner and to the audience. Only when the beginnings, middles, and ends are fully executed is the storytelling potential realized.

BLOCKING

The physical elements of storytelling onstage—movement, gestures, and business. Actors often expect that the director will provide them with their blocking in rehearsals. But as Stanislavski came to believe, the physical choices made by actors are as much a part of the acting as delivering the lines. Those physical actions can tell as much about their characters and about the story as any other acting tool at the performers' disposal. Actors who can act with their bodies as well as with their voices, with or without the director's input, are better actors for the ability. Physical action, as Stanislavski came to believe, can connect actors with their truthful emotional center. But even without that connection, actors who can communicate thought and emotion to an audience through what they physically do are the strongest ones.

BUSINESS

Any ongoing physical activity an actor carries out while pursuing or completing an acting objective onstage. Smoking or drinking are examples of stage business that can add to the actor's characterization and believability—by giving details of the character being played through the manner in which he smokes or drinks. Business is almost always secondary to the main action of the scene and objective of the actor. Like driving a car, business can be executed without direct focusing, unless, of course, the business requires focus for a particular moment—lighting the cigarette, for instance. The specifics of the particular business, however, can help shape a moment or inform an audience of what a character is thinking or feeling. If I choose to drag on my cigarette after being told that my wife has left me, it gives the audience information. The good actor uses business in a specific way to help shape the performance.

CHARACTER

One of Aristotle's basic elements of drama needed in order to have a play. Other elements include dialogue, action, idea, spectacle, and music. We often hear actors talking about "being their characters," "inhabiting their characters," and so on. We also hear about creating biographies of characters' lives before and after the action of the play. All this can be dangerous, especially to a beginning actor. Inhabiting character and living out imaginary biographies can lead actors away from fulfilling their responsibilities to tell the story of the play by making acting choices for their characters that come from the script. Besides, becoming a character may be an illusion, or impossible for some actors to accomplish. Better to focus on the actions of each character and the manner in which those actions are performed. Character is action. When action is combined with externals like costume and makeup, action creates character.

CHOICES

Every actor must make choices about what his character needs from the other characters who surround him, and choices about the tactics to get those needs fulfilled. In real life people seldom think specifically about what they need, or, for that matter, about why they play out many of their actions during the course of the day. Actors, however, must make choices for the characters they play, choices that get them closer to what their characters need, even if the characters themselves are unaware of why they do the things they do. This may sound simplistic, but the fact is when actors make choices that are seemingly too simple, choices that will get them toward their goal, they are making choices that invariably serve the built-in conflict of the plot. Any necessary complexity of character will be provided by the script and the audience's perception of character as they watch the action of the play. Positive choices are ones that help a character get what she needs. Negative choices are choices that do not do so. Actors should play only positive choices. Negative choices make for indulgent and often dull acting—because they diminish or destroy the potential conflict built into a scene by the playwright. Actors should not play their pain. They should acknowledge it and then make new choices that help their character get what they need (fulfill their objectives).

CONFLICT

When two opposing forces meet; the engine of all drama; the core ingredient an actor must recognize before choosing an objective. Playwrights want to tell the best story they possibly can. They know that the good story centers on a conflict—usually between a central character and the obstacles that character faces. Since that is the way plays are structured, actors must be able to recognize the conflict where it exists and then make choices that contribute to that dramatic engine. When actors recognize the conflict in a scene and make their objectives in the scene relate to the other character in the scene who will be opposing the fulfillment of that objective, they contribute to the conflict and to the dramatic success of the scene. Scene by scene, this approach almost guarantees an exciting, watchable story.

CONTEXTUAL MEANING

(See Meaning)

CRAFT

The tools of acting that can be learned and mastered; unlike talent, which is innate and cannot be learned. The mastery of craft can help the gifted actor hone and shape his work. For those less talented, craft can go a long way toward substituting for the lack of natural gifts. Those who choose not to master craft will always have to gamble that their instincts are never wrong and constantly be at the mercy of those who seem to have control of the acting situation. Good directors—directors who are focused on and able to bring out the best in each actor—are hard to find. The actor who has mastered craft need rely only on himself to produce work that gets the job done.

CRITICISM

A necessary part of an actor's work. Without an outside eye to steer the course of an actor's work through critical observation and comment, the actor cannot improve the work she offers. Actors who see criticism as negative, or feel it as such, will have trouble enjoying the creative process and are likely to be difficult to work with. Criticism must be seen as a necessary and positive step toward making the final product the best it can be. Actors who cannot accept criticism naturally must learn to do so quickly. It must be considered part of the craft.

DEFEATS

(See Moments)

DISCOVERIES

(See Moments)

EMOTIONAL MEMORY

The use of personal memory to create an emotion that can be used in an acting situation. This internal approach to acting was discovered and employed by Stanislavski in his early work and described in the book *An Actor Prepares*.

He later abandoned this technique in favor of the external physical approach toward acting he wrote about in his later work. Method acting as described and taught by Lee Strasberg relies heavily on emotional memory—the application of real and honest emotions recalled from past experience and applied to the immediate acting situation.

EMOTIONAL TRUTH

The product of an actor who can find and produce within himself honest emotions that serve the acting situation he is engaged in. At one point Stanislavski felt that emotional truth was best found through the application of **emotional memory**. He later came to feel that emotional truth could better be found as a by-product of physical action that is more reliably repeatable and controllable. Today, most actors accept the validity of both approaches—some relying more heavily on one or the other—although some use one or the other exclusively.

ENDOWMENT

Giving an object specific emotional meaning that can be effectively used for acting purposes. Every prop an actor uses has potential for creating wonderful acting moments—moments that can help communicate how the character is feeling or what she is thinking. When Dorothy picks up the ruby slipper, left by the late witch of the east, for the first time, she does not simply pick it up. She endows the object with the emotion of the moment. When her three friends receive their worthless gifts from the wizard, each endows the objects received with what those objects mean to them, thereby creating wonderful acting moments lasting only seconds onscreen but staying with the audience for the rest of their lives.

EXTERNAL AND INTERNAL

(See Emotional truth and Physical action)

GENRE

The kind of play the author has written, such as drama, comedy, farce, or tragedy. Each type of play has certain characteristics that must be acknowledged and adhered to and may even require a particular style of acting if the play is to be acted effectively. A modern comedy, for instance, is expected to be funny, so the actor must make choices that support the playwright's intention. The actor must try to add to what the playwright has provided and certainly must never diminish what the playwright has offered up as the starting point.

GESTURE

A single specific physical action that communicates emotion, information, or attitude. A choice in a moment of the play to take one's hand and place it on the forehead after hearing that your daughter has died is a gesture. Shaking a fisted hand at an adversary after being embarrassed by him is also a gesture. Each communicates, through its simple execution, information and emotion about the character being played and about the thoughts and feelings of that character. Gestures can be calculated, planned choices that through the rehearsal process become natural and organic, or they may be discovered spontaneously because they actually happen during the rehearsal process or in performance and, because they work, are adopted as part of the performance and used again and again by the actor at that particular moment of the play.

GIVEN CIRCUMSTANCES

The who, what, where, and when of a play or scene that must be considered before making acting choices. When a line is delivered and makes sense in terms of the context of the play, an audience gives it little thought. "Of course, that's the way it should be said," our subconscious would tell us, were we to ask it. It is only when we ask a nonactor to say a particular line that he realizes any line of dialogue could be said an infinite number of ways. Which is right? Which best serves the play? Which best serves the character saying it? Examining the given circumstances of the play, the scene, and the moment helps the actor narrow down the choices. The four W's refer to the *who* (the character saying the line), the *what* (the situation in which she finds herself), the *where* (the location in which this occurs), and the *when* (the time, both general and specific, of the occurrence). Take the line "I love you." How many ways can the line be said? Now narrow down the choices by manipulating the given circumstances. The number remains vast, but you are no longer operating in the dark.

HEAD-FIRST ACTING

A term coined by the author to suggest that good acting requires analysis and synthesis and that the best choices are ones that serve the story. More often than not, these choices must be thought out rather than simply intuited.

INDICATING

When a performer physically demonstrates an action without personal connection to what she is supposed to be thinking, feeling, or doing, thus "indicating" rather than fully committing to the action.

INTENTION

(See Objective)

JOURNEY

(See Action and Arc)

JUSTIFICATION

The process an actor goes through in order to make sure that a line or moment is acted in such a way that it is both believable and clear, and makes sense in terms of the given circumstances of the situation. A line that is not justified will sound wrong or empty when delivered in the context of the play. It will sound like the actor is simply saying the line rather than having a need or

176

purpose for saying it. A playwright puts everything into a script for a reason. An actor must discover those reasons and use these elements to support or enhance what is on the printed page or implied by it.

LISTENING

A basic requirement for an actor if she is to be believed, and an essential step for staying in the moment and reacting effectively. Actors who do not listen may be reliable performers, but their work never varies, seldom grows, and almost never presents the audience or fellow actors with the gift of spontaneity. This freshness will come only as a result of being in the moment. The ability to adjust to the nuances of each new performance keeps an actor's work alive, and the magic found by simply being able to listen and respond to all that is happening in a freshly created moment is the ingredient that can make some actors' work so real and exciting. Those who simply wait their turn to say a line are easily distinguishable from the good actor. So important is this skill that Sanford Meisner devoted much of his teaching to developing this aspect of craft. (See also *Meisner, Sanford.*)

LITERAL MEANING

(See Meaning)

MAGIC IF, THE

An acting term coined by Stanislavski that reminds an actor to ask, "What would I do if I were this character in this situation?" Notice that the question says *do*, not *feel*. Because Stanislavski came to believe that playing out the appropriate actions told the audience more about the character's feelings and thoughts than working with emotion directly, his "magic if" became an essential acting tool. Here is an example. Say you are Laura from *The Glass Menagerie*. You have just been told by Tom, your brother, that your mother, Amanda, has died. What do you do, and what do you feel? Act it now. You may be stuck, especially if you simply try to conjure up some emotional response. But what we know about Laura can give us some good starting clues to actions she might take, which in turn could provide the actor with a springboard for her emotional response. Perhaps Laura would go toward her menagerie to find some comfort. Perhaps she would pick up some pieces and examine them closely. Perhaps she would stroke her favorite one or hold it tightly in her palm while putting it next to her cheek. Character and story can be communicated through what we do and how we do it. Asking "the magic if" can help lead us to those choices.

MEANING

Refers to the three levels of meaning that a line of dialogue may possess. *Literal* meaning refers to what the line means at face value without a context. *Contextual* meaning refers to what the line means in terms of the given circumstances. An "I love you" spoken to a friend who has just thrown you a surprise party means something different than the "I love you" said to a lover during a passionate moment. *Subtextual* meaning refers to dialogue that may hide a much deeper meaning or be used as a filler for thoughts and feelings the speaker does not want to reveal. Anton Chekhov was a master of this kind of dialogue.

MEISNER, SANFORD

One of the great first generation of acting teachers who came from the Group Theatre. Meisner devoted much of his teaching time to finding techniques to better enable his students to listen well and stay in the moment. His most famous exercises are used by countless acting students around the world, whatever approach to acting they are studying. The Meisner repetition games, in which actors repeat what their acting partners say to them and try to turn these repetitions into actual conversations, have become a standard practice highly valued by all who teach and study acting.

METHOD, THE

An internal approach to acting centering on the use of **emotional truth** and **sense memory;** made famous by Lee Strasberg but based primarily on early writings of Stanislavski. Critics of this approach, like Stella Adler, felt the Method was self-indulgent and often made actors look good at the expense of the play. Even she could not argue, however, that the Method was a highly effective technique for film acting, where only a moment might be shot at a time and the intimacy of the camera demanded an emotional presence and honesty not necessarily required by stage acting.

MOMENT

The smallest unit of dramatic action that can be acted. Actors must learn through effective analytical reading and good listening while in rehearsal and performance where moments occur and pick up on the execution of them. Every created moment is an important contribution to the overall story and to the story of each individual character. A fully realized moment has to be clear and full, and most often has a beginning, middle, and end. Moments can occur at any justified time but most often happen at the end of a beat following the delivery of new information, when a discovery is made, or when there is a victory or a defeat in terms of the actor's objective. Any new information an actor as character learns should be reacted to. Examples from *The Glass Menagerie* include when Amanda learns that Tom is planning to leave, or when Laura learns that her mother knows she has not been attending business school. Examples of a discovery are when Olivia realizes why she has been given a ring from the Duke in *Twelfth Night*, or, from *As You Like It*, when Rosalind (disguised as a man) realizes that Phoebe is in love with her. Victories are the actable moments when objectives are reached. When Tom wins the argument about his leaving home and Amanda accepts the fact is a moment (although followed by a transition during which Amanda comes up with a new strategy and new plan of attack). When Jim convinces Laura to join him on the floor of the living room, thereby breaking through her wall of resistance, is a moment of victory, as well. Those same moments are defeats for Amanda and Laura, respectively, and the actors playing them have and should take the opportunity to respond in those moments. These kinds of moments are often followed by moments of transition—equally interesting and equally important to act. (See also **Transitions.**)

MOMENT-TO-MOMENT

Refers to the ability of the good actor to respond to what an acting partner is saying and doing at a particular moment. Moment-to-moment acting requires good listening and is essential for believability, for spontaneity, and for the discovery of actions that can define a moment.

MOTIVATION

The reason behind a character pursuing a particular objective. Motivation cannot be played directly but can be used as a device to find the acting objective that can and must be played at every moment of a character's stage life. Here is an example. I am jealous of my brother. My mother always liked him better. How do I play jealous? I cannot. But I can try to hurt him whenever possible—to get back at him for taking all of our mother's love. Jealousy is the motivation; punishing my brother is my objective. I can and should play my objective.

MOVEMENT

The aspect of blocking when an actor travels from one place to another onstage. An actor should never make purposeless movements. An actor crosses the stage because his character needs to put distance between himself and another character, or because he needs to cut down the distance between them. If an actor chooses to move away from someone or something, he is also moving toward someone or something else—with purpose. These movements have beginnings, middles, and ends, and the character should acknowledge these steps onstage to help him communicate his thoughts and feelings. Any movement should be connected to the actor's particular objective at any given time. Since physical positioning can help a character get what he needs or keep another character from getting what she needs, the physical relationship between characters onstage should be used to establish or maintain power and weakness that tie into a character's objective. The good actor is aware of this and uses this tool to pursue his purpose and help reveal his inner life to the watching audience.

NEGATIVE CHOICES

(See Choices)

NEW INFORMATION

(See Choices)

OBJECTIVES

The needs an actor playing a character must pursue at all times onstage. Acting is not the same as life; it just closely resembles it when well done. No matter how well the actor probes the psyche and emotions of a character from the printed page, to some extent the actor is pretending. His words are not his own; they are borrowed from the playwright, who has written them for just this purpose. In life a person's actions are often random, and where they will lead, a person never fully knows until they are played out. Life is messy, often leaving many loose ends. A character in a play, on the other hand, is a creation resulting from the imagination of a playwright with the power to select and control the actions of that character—so that they play out in accordance with the action of the play being written. It follows, then, that a character's behavior is simpler by far than that of a living, breathing person. Each choice, each action the actor as character makes and plays must therefore support the track the playwright has laid out. By pursuing the goal of the character, whether that character is aware of that goal or not, the actor creates the illusion of reality while making choices that ultimately serve the story of the character and of the play. Most objectives should be connected to the other characters who share a scene. Chances are that if a playwright put two characters in a scene, the conflict lies between those characters. The objective—to win something from that other character—most often arises from that conflict.

OBSTACLES

The elements in a scene or play that keep a character from obtaining his objective. They provide conflict and heighten the stakes of any acting situation. These obstacles can be in the form of another character (Tybalt for Romeo). They can be internal (the struggle within Friar Lawrence to decide whether he should perform the marriage rites for Romeo and Juliet). They can be external (the politics of Nazi Germany that infuses *The Diary of Anne Frank*). Or they can be inanimate (the weather in *The Grapes of Wrath*). Whatever the category, obstacles help keep the actions of a character and the overall story of a play interesting and exciting. Ask yourself what obstacles Laura in *The Glass Menagerie* faces — internally, from another character, and as a result of the given circumstances of the play. Now do the same for Tom, Amanda, and the "gentleman caller." Notice how these obstacles lend both the characters and the story heightened interest. The actor must look for these obstacles in the script and use them to make his journey through the story as exciting as possible.

PHYSICAL ACTION

The tangible and visible things a character does onstage. Try playing anger directly. Take a moment now and try to conjure anger. Did you feel it? Would I recognize this feeling were I an audience watching? Now make a fist and slam it on a table as though you were angry. Did you fully commit to the action? If you did, you probably felt anger. The audience watching probably would have recognized your action as anger, as well. Now plan a sequence of actions that tells a story and that communicates what you are thinking and feeling. Make your physical planning specific, and rehearse each action carefully in sequence. When you have done so, you are acting in the manner that Stanislavski describes in his later work. This kind of approach to acting is clear, interesting, controllable, and repeatable. So is the good actor's work.

POSITIVE CHOICES

(See Choices)

PSYCHOLOGICAL ACTION

(See Action)

RISK

A basic tool for producing interesting acting; the more risk taken, the more interesting the actor in a situation. Another term for this concept is *the big choice*. What makes you the more interesting actor—simply doing what is believable, or making the most interesting believable choice possible? The actor who takes risks and does so in a believable manner is the one who get jobs—because she is the one who produces the most watchable work. The acting moments best remembered are the ones where the actor surprises you yet you recognize the rightness of the choice.

SENSE MEMORY

The use of personal memory relating to smell, sound, taste, touch, and sight to enhance the emotional power of an acting moment or situation. The actor who must smell the imaginary flower onstage will enhance his work by recalling specifically the beautiful fragrance of a flower actually smelled. Sense memories are among the strongest we possess. We can often remember the moment we actually heard a song for the first time, the smell of the house we grew up in at dinnertime, the taste of the first lobster we ever ate. An actor must make real for himself all that he does onstage and find ways to communicate those things to an audience. By leading himself to precise moments in such memories of sense, he can apply what he discovers to the current acting work being portrayed.

STAKES

What is at risk for the actor as character as she pursues her objective? These discovered *stakes* can help the actor make the acting situation as interesting as possible. As Amanda pressures Tom to bring home a suitor for Laura (*The Glass Menagerie*), what is at risk for her? As Laura comes out of her shell to meet the expectations and pressure of her gentleman caller, what does she risk? When Romeo climbs the orchard wall, or when Juliet agrees to meet her new lover at Friar Lawrence's cell, what is each risking? In all of these cases, the characters are willing to chance an enormous amount in order to get what they want. Awareness of what is at stake keeps the danger factor high for the actor and tells the audience quite a bit about the characters they are playing. Finding the stakes in the situations less obviously risky is a more difficult trick. But since plays tell stories filled with conflict, the playwright has stuffed them with huge risk potential. It is up to the actor to find the high stakes and use them to make the work as exciting as it can possibly be.

STANISLAVSKI, KONSTANTIN

The Russian theatre director, actor, and teacher responsible for most of the basic craft used in actor training. During his more than fifty-year exploration of the acting process, he developed theories and strategies, internal and external, that remain the cornerstones for acting craft today.

STRASBERG, LEE

The most famous of the great seminal American acting teachers, Strasberg developed "the Method," employed by many of the great realistic film actors of the postwar era.

STYLE

Simply put, the world of the play. Actors must know the world of the play in which they are performing and make choices in thought and action that are consistent with those of the other actors in the play and with the world created by the playwright. Realism, for instance, though referred to as an acting style, really refers to the kind of world created by the playwright — a world that seems very much like the one we inhabit in our own contemporary life. American plays of the 1930s such as *Awake and Sing!* were examples of realism in the time they were written. Today, their language no longer represents what we consider realism. But they present a consistent world throughout. The actor must understand and find a way to act believably within that world.

SUBSTITUTION

A technique in which an actor substitutes a parallel personal memory from his own life for a similar one in the play she is working on to enhance her emotional connection to a moment. Often used by Strasberg in his "Method" approach to acting. Though Stanislavski developed it, he later abandoned its use. Stella Adler found substitution to be a ridiculously distracting approach to an acting problem because it separated the actor from being in the moment of the play.

SUBTEXTUAL MEANING

(See Meaning)

TACTICS

The specific strategies an actor as character uses while pursuing her objective. Some acting teachers break down objectives into smaller units when analyzing a script. These are usually referred to as *tactics*. For instance, your objective is to get your father to let you use the car tonight. He is against the idea. How many approaches can you come up with to get the car before your father finally gives in to you? Make a list of your strategies. Those are your tactics. You use them one at a time until you accomplish your objective and get your father to put the keys in your hand. In a scene, an actor as character often goes through the same process, whether planned or spontaneously. Each strategy is a tactic employed until there is a recognition that the tactic has succeeded or failed, at which time another is thought up and employed, and then another — until your objective is fulfilled or abandoned.

THROUGHLINE

(See Arc)

TRANSITIONS

The actable moments when one objective is given up and replaced with another. A transition occurs as a result of an objective being lost, won, or abandoned because of new information, an interruption, or a discovery. Often the transitional moment provides the actor with a wonderful opportunity to show the audience what she is thinking or feeling. Sometimes, however, the rapid switch to a new tactic or objective without hesitation can be extremely interesting, but only if the audience understands the jump. Here are some examples. You have been pressuring your father for the keys to his car. He gives them to you, and a victory moment is played, followed by the finding of a new objective—to get him to give you gas money. Your father threatens that if you say one thing more on the subject of car keys he will ground you for a month—a defeat. While you are sweet-talking your father, there is a phone call for you and you find out that Billy got his dad's car for the evening—new information that changes the situation. During your tactical advance on Dad, your mother enters with news that Aunt Joan has been in a car accident—an interruption and new information that changes the situation completely. While Dad is denying your advances, he is very funny and charming. You realize that you would rather stay home with the family than go out—a discovery that forces you into a transitional moment.

VICTORIES

(See Moments)

BIBLIOGRAPHY

Aristotle. *Poetics.* Trans. Kenneth A. Telford. Chicago: Gateway, 1968.

Ball, David. *Backwards and Forwards.* Carbondale: Southern Illinois University Press, 1983.

Barranger, Millie. *Theatre—A Way of Seeing.* Belmont, Calif.: Wadsworth, 1995.

Barton, Robert. *Style for Actors.* Mountain View, Calif.: Mayfield, 1993.

Brook, Peter. *The Empty Space.* New York: Atheneum, 1968.

Bruder, Melissa, et al. *A Practical Handbook for the Actor.* New York: Vintage Press, 1986.

Cohen, Robert. *Acting One.* Palo Alto, Calif.: Mayfield, 1984

Cohen, Robert. *Acting Power.* Palo Alto, Calif.: Mayfield, 1978.

Cohen, Robert, and John Harrop. *Creative Play Direction.* Englewood Cliffs, N.J.: Prentice-Hall, 1974.

Donnellan, Declan. *The Actor and the Target.* New York: Theatre Communications Group, 206.

Felnagle, Richard H. *Beginning Acting.* Englewood Cliffs, N.J.: Prentice-Hall, 1987.

Fingerhut, Arden. *Theatre—Choice in Action.* New York: Harper Collins College, 1995.

Grote, David. *Script Analysis.* Belmont, Calif.: Wadsworth, 1985.

Hagen, Uta. *Respect for Acting.* New York: Macmillan, 1973.

Hornby, Richard. *The End of Acting.* New York: Applause Books, 1992.

Kirk, John W., and Ralph A. Bellas. *The Art of Direction.* Hudson, Ill.: Ad Hoc Productions, 1989.

Shurtleff, Michael. *Audition: Everything an Actor Needs to Know to Get the Part.* New York: Walker, 1978.

Stanislavski, Constantin. *An Actor Prepares.* Trans. Elizabeth Reynolds Hapgood. New York: Theatre Arts Books, 1936

Stanislavski, Constantin. *Building a Character.* Trans. Elizabeth Reynolds Hapgood. New York: Theatre Arts Books, 1949.

Stanislavski, Constantin. *Creating a Role.* Trans. Elizabeth Reynolds Hapgood. New York: Theatre Arts Books, 1961.

Thomas, James. *Script Analysis for Actors, Directors, and Designers.* Boston: Focal Press, 1999.

Waxberg, Charles. *The Actor's Script.* Portsmouth, N.H.: Heinemann, 1998.